Data Leader

A PRACTICAL GUIDE TO BUILDING AND LEADING A DATA ORGANIZATION AT ANY LEVEL

Steven Jordan

Technics Publications
SEDONA, ARIZONA

TECHNICS PUBLICATIONS

115 Linda Vista, Sedona, AZ 86336 USA
https://www.TechnicsPub.com

Edited by Steve Hoberman
Cover design by Lorena Molinari

First Printing 2026

ISBN, print ed. 9798898161651
ISBN, Kindle ed. 9798898161668
ISBN, PDF ed. 9798898161675

For Allyson, William, and Hannah.

Thank you for putting up with my incessant need to talk about data, leadership, and this book for years. I could not have written it without your patience and support.

Contents

Preface

In 2006, British mathematician and data entrepreneur Clive Humby coined a phrase that would ricochet around boardrooms and conference slides for the next two decades: "Data is the new oil." The slogan spread so cleanly and so fast that the rest of what was said that day almost immediately disappeared. Michael Palmer, then executive vice president of the Association of National Advertisers, expanded on Humby's idea in a blog post published on November 3, 2006, writing: "Data is just like crude. It's valuable, but if unrefined it cannot really be used. It has to be changed into gas, plastic, chemicals, etc. to create a valuable entity that drives profitable activity; so must data be broken down, analyzed for it to have value."[1]

That second part matters. And it is almost always left out.

Organizations have spent the better part of two decades collecting and storing data at extraordinary scale. Many of them are still sitting on the unrefined version. The gap between the data that organizations have and the value they can generate from it is not primarily a technology problem. RAND Corporation's 2024 study of enterprise data and AI programs, based on structured interviews with 65 experienced data scientists and engineers, found that more than 80% of AI projects fail, roughly double the

1 Michael Palmer, "Data Is the New Oil," ANA Marketing Maestros (blog), Association of National Advertisers, November 3, 2006.

failure rate of non-AI IT projects, and that the highest-impact causes are not technical limitations. They are misaligned incentives, absent leadership sponsorship, poor problem framing, and a failure to involve end users in design.[2] Gartner's research has reached similar conclusions across multiple studies spanning more than a decade, with analysts repeatedly finding that people, process, and culture outweigh technology as the dominant driver of failure. Year after year, the NewVantage Partners surveys of C-suite executives at major corporations have found that more than 90% of respondents identify cultural and organizational challenges, not technology, as the primary obstacle to becoming data-driven.[3]

The conversation about why data initiatives fail rarely focuses on the most important variable: leadership.

This book is an attempt to change that conversation.

I did not come to data leadership through a traditional path, and I suspect many of you did not either. My first leadership experience came at nineteen years old in the United States Army, where I became a team leader of infantry soldiers in the Army's

[2] **Preface:** RAND Corporation, "The Root Causes of Failure for Artificial Intelligence Projects" (Santa Monica, CA: RAND Corporation, 2024), report no. RRA2680-1, based on structured interviews with 65 data scientists and engineers.

[3] NewVantage Partners, now published as the Wavestone AI & Data Leadership Executive Benchmark Survey, an annual survey of Fortune 1000 data and AI leaders conducted since 2012.

Old Guard. The Army takes leadership seriously in a way that few institutions do, and those early lessons about accountability, clarity of mission, and taking care of the people in your charge have never left me.

From the Army, I briefly moved into leading airline customer service agents, which was a culture shock of the most instructive kind. Leading union employees in a difficult customer-facing environment taught me that authority means very little without trust. You cannot order people to do anything in the civilian world, and especially not in that one. The only currency that works is influence, built through relationship and consistency over time.

My data career came next, bringing a third education. For years, I supported senior operations leaders as a data analyst at large companies, and watching how the best of them operated shaped how I eventually led data teams. Their obsession with process, their intolerance for inefficiency, and their insistence on measuring what mattered became the operating principles I carried into every data leadership role that followed.

For the past decade, I have had the privilege of leading data professionals across industries, building data organizations from the ground up, and navigating every challenge this book covers. The politics of getting a data strategy funded, the difficulty of hiring in a market where talent is scarce and expectations are high, the frustration of delivering real business value and watching it go unnoticed, and the specific loneliness of leading a function that most of the organization does not fully understand.

Several years ago, I proposed and built a graduate course at the University of North Carolina at Charlotte called "Building and Leading Data Organizations." Designing that course forced me to do something my day job never quite required: take everything I knew about this field, combined with a significant amount of research into what the best practitioners and organizations had learned, and organize it into a coherent framework that someone with no prior experience could follow from beginning to end. The course worked. And the process of building it revealed, more clearly than anything else I had done, exactly how much useful knowledge existed in scattered form and how little of it had been assembled in one place. This book is that assembly.

I am not writing this book because I believe I have mastered this field. I am writing it because it is the book I wanted when I started.

When I became a data leader, I searched for something that would explain what functions a data organization needs, how to build a strategy that connects to the business, how to develop processes that make work repeatable, and how to lead people doing work that most of the organization cannot evaluate. I did not find it. There were books on data architecture, data governance, and analytics strategy, but nothing that held the full picture together from a leader's perspective.

Data is an unusual field. It sits at the crossroads of business and technology in a way that creates extraordinary demands on the people who lead it. Data leaders are expected to understand the

business they support nearly as well as their business partners do, understand information systems and IT strategy nearly as well as their IT partners do, stay current on a technology landscape that reinvents itself every few years, manage and develop highly specialized technical talent, and translate all of it into language that makes sense to executives who control the budget. None of that is a complaint. It's some of the most challenging and rewarding work I have done. But it does mean that new leaders in this field face a steeper learning curve than almost any comparable role.

It also means that feeling like you do not know enough is the norm. Research published in the *Journal of General Internal Medicine* has found that imposter phenomenon, the persistent sense that you have not earned your place despite evidence to the contrary, affects people across professional settings, with high rates in high-achieving environments.[4] Ruchika Tulshyan and Jodi-Ann Burey, writing in the *Harvard Business Review* in 2021, made the important point that what gets labeled as imposter syndrome is often less a personal failing and more a rational response to difficult circumstances, environments that are new, fast-changing, and where the definition of success keeps shifting.[5] That description fits the data profession precisely. Chief Data Officer (CDO) tenure remains notoriously short by executive

---

[4] Dena M. Bravata et al., "Prevalence, Predictors, and Treatment of Impostor Syndrome: A Systematic Review," Journal of General Internal Medicine 35, no. 4 (2020): 1252–75.

[5] Ruchika Tulshyan and Jodi-Ann Burey, "Stop Telling Women They Have Imposter Syndrome," Harvard Business Review, February 11, 2021.

standards, often cited in the two- to three-year range, and a meaningful share of CDO hires are considered unsuccessful by the organizations that make them. The field is hard. The ambiguity is real. Feeling uncertain is not evidence that you do not belong. It is evidence that you are paying attention.

I hope that this book helps with that. Not by pretending the job is simpler than it is, but by revealing a truth. Nobody knows everything about leading in data. The field is too new, too broad, and too fast-moving for any single person to have mastered all of it. What the best data leaders share is not comprehensive expertise. It is a framework for thinking about the work, a clear-eyed view of what the function requires, and the humility to keep learning.

The chapters ahead cover the full arc of building and leading a data organization. What each major function is and why it exists, how to build a strategy that connects to what the business cares about, how to develop processes that make good work repeatable, how to hire and lead the people who do that work, how to measure and communicate the value the organization creates, and how to prepare for a field that will look meaningfully different in five years than it does today. No single chapter will make you an expert in its subject. Each subject is a career in itself. But the goal is not to be an expert in every domain. The goal is the kind of informed leadership that allows you to build something that works.

I am grateful you're here. Let's get to work.

Introduction

There is a moment I think about often when I try to explain why I ended up in this field.

I was in my mid-twenties, working as an airport vendor manager at American Airlines. My job was to improve the performance of the vendors who handled baggage and customer service at smaller regional airports across the country. I had about six months of airport experience at that point. I was, to put it plainly, completely out of my depth. I did not have the operational expertise to walk into an airport and tell experienced managers what they were doing wrong. I did not have the tenure to command authority. What I had was data.

I started pulling together reports and analyses and sending them to the leaders at each airport: on-time performance by shift and baggage-handling error rates by time of day. Simple stuff, by today's standards. Their responses shocked me.

They had no idea.

These were experienced operations managers who had been running their airports for years. Nobody had ever shown them their own numbers in a way that was clear and actionable. When I sent a report showing that the night shift on weekends accounted for the majority of errors, they could see it and respond immediately. Performance improved. Not because I told them what to do. Because I gave them information they could act on.

That experience sent me down a path I have been on ever since, going deeper into the world of data and what it can do when it is organized, communicated, and led well. It also planted a question that this book is my best attempt to answer. Why does something so valuable remain so mismanaged, underutilized, and misunderstood inside most organizations?

The answer, I have come to believe, is not technology. It is leadership. More specifically, it is the lack of a clear picture of what it takes to lead a data organization.

What This Book Is About

Data Leader is a practical guide to building and leading modern data organizations. It covers the full arc of the work. From understanding what each major function of a data organization is and why it exists, building a strategy that connects to business outcomes, developing processes that make good work repeatable, hiring and leading the people who do that work, measuring and communicating the value the organization creates, and preparing for a field that is changing faster than any single book can fully capture.

The organizing premise is straightforward. Before you can build a data organization, you need to understand what one is. Before you can lead one, you need to know what it takes to build one. And before you can sustain one, you need to be able to measure and communicate its value in terms the business cares about. The book follows that sequence: understand, build, and lead.

This book is not a technical manual. There are no code samples. There are no deep dives into specific tools or platforms. The technology changes too quickly for any book to keep pace with it across the data landscape, and more importantly, mastery of specific tools is not what separates good data leaders from great ones. What separates them is the ability to think clearly about organizational problems, communicate across technical and business boundaries, and make decisions in conditions of genuine ambiguity. Those are the skills this book is designed to develop.

The Thesis

Most data initiatives fail not because of inadequate technology but because of inadequate leadership. The models are good enough. The infrastructure is accessible enough. What is missing in most organizations that struggle with data is the organizational capability to refine raw data into decisions that drive business outcomes, supported by a clear strategy, sound processes, the right talent, effective governance, and leaders who understand both the technical landscape and the business context well enough to connect them.

This book is built around the belief that those capabilities can be learned, and that the leaders who develop them will build data organizations that consistently deliver value rather than consistently promising it.

Who This Book Is For

This book is written for three distinct audiences, and each will get something different from it.

Data professionals currently working in data organizations, whether as individual contributors or early-stage leaders, will find in this book a framework for understanding the full scope of the function they are part of. If you have spent your career becoming an expert in one domain, whether analytics or engineering or governance, this book will give you a clear picture of how your work fits into the larger system and what it looks like to lead it. It is also written for the data professional who is eyeing a leadership role and wants to understand what that transition requires.

Students and aspiring data professionals who are preparing to enter the field will find in this book an honest orientation to how data organizations work, what the major roles and functions are, and what the career landscape looks like. The field is new enough that most educational programs do not yet cover this material. This book is designed to fill that gap.

Business and IT leaders who work alongside data organizations but do not sit inside them will find in this book the clearest possible explanation of what the data function is, what it requires to succeed, and what the people leading it are trying to accomplish. If you have ever struggled to evaluate a data leader's request for budget, to understand why a data initiative is taking longer than expected, or to assess whether your organization's data function is performing at the level it should be, this book is written with you in mind.

The technical prerequisites are minimal. This book assumes a basic familiarity with what data is and why it matters, but it does not assume expertise in any specific tool, platform, or methodology. Readers who have spent years working with SQL and machine learning will find the technical concepts familiar; readers who have spent their careers in business leadership will find nothing that requires a technical background to understand.

How to Read This Book

The book is organized into three modules that follow a deliberate sequence.

Part 1: Laying the Foundation covers the major functional areas of a data organization: data governance, data management, data architecture, data engineering, business intelligence, analytics, data science, and artificial intelligence. If you are new to the field or want to fill gaps in your understanding of functions outside your specialty, read Part 1 in sequence. If you are an experienced data professional who already has a clear picture of the landscape, you may want to skim or selectively read the chapters that cover territory less familiar to you.

Part 2: Building Data Organizations covers how to build a data strategy, develop the processes that allow a data organization to operate consistently, and hire the talent needed to execute.

Part 3: Leading Data Organizations covers the full human side of running a data organization: leading and developing data talent, building the stakeholder relationships that determine whether the function can accomplish anything beyond its own walls, navigating the organizational change that data transformation requires, scaling the function as it grows, measuring and communicating the value of data work, and preparing for where the field is heading.

Legacy Paper and Supply

Each chapter in this book closes with a section called "Legacy Paper and Supply." Legacy is a fictional regional paper and office supply distributor that appears throughout the book as a running case study. At the end of each chapter, we follow a data leader who has just joined Legacy and is applying the chapter's concepts to a real organizational situation, working toward specific business goals.

Legacy is not Amazon or Google. It does not have unlimited resources, a world-class data team, or a culture that is already data driven. It is a company that looks a lot like the organizations most data leaders work in, and the challenges it faces are the ones most data leaders are trying to solve. The goal of the Legacy sections is not to provide a perfect template but to give the book's concepts a concrete home where you can see how they play out in conditions that feel recognizable, and how every decision, from governance policy to hiring choice to architectural pattern, connects back to business outcomes that matter.

A Note on the Field

Data is a young discipline. The Chief Data Officer role did not exist in meaningful numbers until the early 2010s. Many of the frameworks and practices this book covers are still being defined and debated. Standards that exist today will look different in five years. Tools that are dominant right now may not be dominant in the next edition of this book.

This means two things for the reader. First, you should hold the specific recommendations in this book with appropriate flexibility. The principles are more durable than the particulars. Second, and more importantly, you should feel some relief. Nobody in this field has it fully figured out. The most common reason data organizations struggle is not that their leaders lack intelligence or effort. It is that the field has not yet produced a sufficient body of shared knowledge about what good data leadership looks like.

That body of knowledge is being built right now, by the people reading books like this one. You are not behind. You are early.

PART I

Laying the Foundation

Before you can build a data organization, you need to know what one is.

That sounds obvious. In practice, it is where many data leaders quietly struggle.

Some arrive with deep technical expertise in one or two of these functions and only a working knowledge of the rest. The data scientist who becomes a manager realizes she does not fully understand what a data governance program does. The analytics director who takes on a broader data leadership role discovers that data architecture and data engineering, which had always seemed like one thing, are two distinct disciplines with different owners, tools, and organizational dynamics.

Others arrive from the opposite direction; they have real leadership experience, built in sales, operations, IT, or another part of the business entirely, but minimal exposure to data specifically. The VP of Sales Operations asked to also take ownership of the data function knows exactly how to run a team, manage a budget, and navigate the Chief Financial Officer's (CFO's) expectations. What she does not yet know is that "the data team" is not one discipline needing one kind of oversight. It is six, each with its own tools, failure modes, and vocabulary.

Both paths lead to the same first year, discovering how much you did not know about the functions you were not trained in.

Part 1 closes that gap. The six chapters ahead cover the core functions of a modern data organization. Each chapter explains what the function is, introduces the concepts and tools a leader needs to understand, addresses the failure modes most organizations encounter, and closes with a section on Legacy Paper and Supply, where you will see how the concepts play out in a concrete organizational situation.

A few things to keep in mind as you read.

The goal is not expertise. As we mentioned before, each of these disciplines is a career in its own right. You are not trying to master any of them. You are trying to develop enough fluency to ask intelligent questions, make good decisions, and support the people who do go deep. There is a meaningful difference between those two things, and this module is aimed at fluency, not mastery.

The functions are interdependent. Data management cannot succeed without governance. Data engineering builds on the architectural blueprint. Analytics depends on what engineering makes available. Data science depends on what analytics has established. The chapters are organized to reflect those dependencies, and you will see each function build on the ones that came before it in the Legacy narrative.

The technical details here are the minimum a leader needs. If you want to go deeper on any of these areas, there is a rich body of practitioner literature for each one. This module gives you the map. Other books give you the terrain.

Let's begin.

ONE

Modern Data Organizations

What Is Data?

If we are going to build data organizations, we need to start with the most basic question. What exactly is data?

Merriam-Webster defines it as "factual information used as a basis for reasoning, discussion, or calculation." That works, but I find it more useful to think of data as the raw material of information.

> *If coal, iron, and timber fueled the Industrial Revolution, then data and computational bandwidth are fueling the information and AI revolution of our time.*

In their raw form, they are just ingredients. Organized, prepared, and combined with skill, they become something useful.

You can scarcely move through modern life without creating data. Every purchase you make, every website you visit, every show you stream. Almost everything you do generates a data point. That data is collected, moved between systems, organized, stored, and eventually analyzed by data professionals working behind the scenes. Companies that learn to responsibly harness that data earn competitive advantages, build better products, and make smarter decisions.

What Is a Data Organization?

For the purposes of this book, a data organization consists of the functions and people that must work together to ensure data is leveraged to meet an organization's broader goals.

That definition matters. It does not say "the data team" or "the analytics department." A data organization is often not a single team. It is a collection of closely related functions, each with a distinct purpose, that depend on each other to deliver value. In a mature organization, those functions include: Data Governance, Data Management, Data Architecture, Data Engineering, Business Intelligence, Analytics, Data Science, and AI.

These are different disciplines. They require different skill sets, different tools, and different ways of thinking. But they are deeply interdependent. When they work well together, the whole is greater than the sum of the parts. When they do not, the result is exactly the kind of dysfunction that produces failed initiatives and frustrated executives.

Here is a brief orientation to each function:

Data Governance is the framework of policies, standards, roles, and processes that determines who owns data, who can access it, how it is protected, and how it is used responsibly. Think of governance as the rules of the road. Without it, everyone is driving however they want, and the accidents are inevitable.

Data Management ensures that data is accurate, complete, consistent, and accessible. This function implements the processes and structures that govern how data is organized, stored, and integrated across systems.

Data Architecture is the blueprint for how data flows through the organization, from creation to the point where it drives a decision. Data architects define the structure, standards, and models that ensure data moves efficiently and serves the business.

Data Engineering is the infrastructure layer. Data engineers build and maintain the pipelines that collect, move, store, and process data at scale. Without solid engineering underneath, there is nothing for analysts, scientists, or business leaders to use.

Business Intelligence and Analytics is where data becomes information. BI analysts build the reports and dashboards that help leaders understand what is happening. Data analysts investigate specific business questions and translate findings into recommendations the business can act on. Analytics engineers sit at the intersection of engineering and analytics, building the clean, reliable data models that everyone else depends on.

Data Science and Artificial Intelligence is where information becomes insight and, increasingly, where insight becomes action. Data scientists build predictive and prescriptive models that anticipate what will happen next. Machine learning engineers operationalize those models, moving them from experimentation into production systems that run at scale. As AI capabilities expand, this function is taking on a broader role in how organizations automate decisions and generate value from their data.

What Value Do Data Organizations Add?

Here is what a well-run data organization delivers. It drives better decisions by turning raw data into actionable information. It powers systems that act without anyone making a decision at all: a fraud model that blocks a transaction, a pricing engine that adjusts in real time, a pipeline that simply keeps running. It improves operational efficiency by identifying bottlenecks and opportunities that are not visible to the naked eye. It mitigates risk by ensuring data is accurate, secure, and compliant with regulations before problems become liabilities. And it creates competitive advantage by enabling the business to understand its customers, markets, and operations more deeply than competitors can.

But here is the problem data leaders face, and you will encounter it within your first six months. Most of the value the data organization creates is invisible.

Think of it as an iceberg. What senior leadership sees above the waterline is the marketing campaign that drove a 12% increase in sales. What they do not see beneath the surface is everything that made that campaign possible: the data scientists who built the segmentation models, the analysts who designed and measured the campaign, the data architects who designed the underlying infrastructure, the data engineers who sourced and transformed the raw data, the data management team that ensured accuracy and accessibility, and the governance team that created the compliance processes that made it all permissible to use. The marketing team gets the credit, and often the budget.

This is one of the defining challenges of data leadership: building something whose value is structurally hidden from the people who control the resources. It is also one of the reasons data initiatives get defunded when budgets tighten. Sales and marketing are seen as value generators. Data and IT are seen as cost centers. Changing that narrative is a survival skill.

We will spend an entire chapter on measuring and communicating the value of data in Part 3. But I want to name it here, at the very beginning, because it shapes everything about how you should think and operate. You are building a case, every single day, for why this function deserves to exist and grow.

How Big Does A Data Organization Need to Be?

The six functions just described exist in every organization that uses data, whether anyone has drawn org chart boxes around them or not. What varies enormously is how many people are doing that work, whether the functions are separate at all, and how much specialization has developed within each one.

At one extreme, one person does all six, informally, often without realizing that's what they're doing. A single analyst at a fifty-person company might spend Monday cleaning a spreadsheet (data management), Tuesday deciding who should have access to it (governance), Wednesday building a script to automate the cleaning (engineering), and Thursday presenting what it all means to the CEO (analytics). Nobody calls this a data organization. It is one, just an extremely compressed one, existing entirely inside a single person's calendar.

At the other extreme, a large enterprise runs six separate departments, each with its own director or VP, its own hiring pipeline, its own specialized tools, and often further specialization within the function itself. Data engineering alone might split into platform engineering, which builds and maintains the infrastructure, and analytics engineering, which builds the models everyone else queries. Data science might split into research scientists exploring what is possible and applied machine learning engineers who ship what already works into production Each sub-team could report up through its own function to a CDO or CDAO (Chief Data and Analytics Officer), the only person in the organization whose job is to see all six functions as one coordinated system rather than six departments that happen to share a budget line.

There is no fixed headcount where a company crosses from one stage to the next. What matters is not where the org chart currently draws its boxes. It is whether all six functions are happening, however informally, and whether the people doing them understand which function they are operating in at any given moment.

Joining a fifty-person company as a data leader usually means building most of these functions from something close to nothing. Joining a five-thousand-person company usually means inheriting functions that already exist, a genuinely different problem to solve. Legacy Paper and Supply, the company you are about to spend the rest of this book with, sits much closer to the first situation than the second.

How Are Data Organizations Structured?

A common question new data leaders face is: How should our data organization be structured?

The honest answer is that it depends on context, and there is a more important thing to understand before getting into models. Organizational structure exists on a spectrum, not as a set of fixed categories. Think of it as a dial running from fully decentralized on one end to fully centralized on the other. Most organizations do not sit cleanly at either extreme, and most shift position over time as their needs and maturity change. Companies regularly move between more centralized and more decentralized structures in response to growth, cost pressure, or a new executive with a different philosophy.

Centralized organizations consolidate all data functions under a single leader, typically a Chief Data Officer (CDO) or Chief Data and Analytics Officer (CDAO), with a unified team serving the entire enterprise. The advantages are consistency, shared standards, and clear accountability. The challenges are speed and business alignment. A centralized team serving many business units can feel slow and disconnected, leaving partners feeling their needs are perpetually in a queue behind everyone else's.

Decentralized organizations distribute data ownership to individual business units. Marketing owns marketing data, while operations owns operations data. This model enables speed and domain expertise but tends to lead to duplicated effort, inconsistent standards, and data that cannot be easily combined across the enterprise.

Hybrid organizations combine elements of both, and this is where most mature organizations land. A central team handles shared infrastructure, governance standards, and platform management. Embedded data professionals within business units do the contextual, day-to-day work. This structure is sometimes called hub-and-spoke. The hub manages the platform and sets the standards; the spokes execute within their domains. This is where most medium- to large-sized enterprises land.

The reality of data leadership authority. One structural reality about data organizations rarely gets named directly: the data team has no formal authority over the business units it exists to serve. Unlike finance, which can require compliance with accounting standards, or legal, which can block a contract, the data organization cannot compel anyone to use its dashboards, follow its governance policies, or trust its models. Everything the data team delivers depends on voluntary adoption.

This makes data leadership fundamentally different from most other functional leadership roles. Influence, trust, and relationship-building are not soft skills that round out a technical leader. They are the primary mechanisms through which a data organization creates value. By understanding this early, you will build, communicate, and prioritize differently.

Three broader ideas to carry through the rest of this book:

- **Organizations are social systems before they are technical systems.** The best data platform in the world will fail if the people it is supposed to serve do not trust it, do not understand it, or feel like it was built without their input. Adoption is not automatic. It has to be earned.

- **Data organizations are almost always change agents.** You are asking the rest of the business to work differently. To consult data before making decisions, to follow governance processes they have never had to follow before, to trust a model instead of their gut. Change is uncomfortable, and people resist it in ways that feel irrational from the outside. Understanding why resistance happens and how to address it is an important leadership skill in this field.

- **Alignment with business goals matters more than almost anything else**. The most effective data organizations are not the ones with the most sophisticated technology stacks. They are the ones most connected to what the business needs. Translating business objectives into data priorities, and translating data capabilities back into business outcomes, is the core skill of data leadership.

Further Reading

Foundational works for going deeper on this topic:

The Data-Driven Leader by Sandro Saitta, an approachable, jargon-free grounding in data and AI for anyone who isn't already a specialist, useful context before the functional chapters that follow.

The Data Asset: How Smart Companies Govern Their Data for Business Success by Tony Fisher, an early and still-relevant case for treating data as a managed organizational asset, the premise this whole book builds on.

Legacy Paper and Supply: You Were Just Hired

Senior leadership at Legacy Paper and Supply brought you in with a seemingly simple mandate: build a data organization to help the company leverage its data more effectively. They shook your hand, showed you to your desk, and walked out of the room. Now you are sitting there wondering where on earth to start.

Everyone who has ever done this job started in exactly that chair, wondering the same thing. The temptation runs in two directions. A new leader will often jump straight into the day-to-day work of the team, fixing whatever is in front of them. A more experienced leader will often retreat into planning. Building a strategy, planning a transition to the cloud, looking at what roles to hire. You take a third path: you start asking questions. In doing so, you learn important information that shapes everything else you do in the role.

Legacy Paper and Supply is a fictional regional paper and office supply distributor based in the mid-Atlantic United States. This company has been in business for over 40 years, and was built on strong customer relationships and a reputation for reliability. It has five regional branches, roughly 200 employees, and a loyal but slowly shrinking customer base with roughly $80 million in annual revenue. Digital communication has been eating into paper demand for years, and larger national competitors with sophisticated online platforms are undercutting Legacy on price and convenience. Leadership has finally decided it is time to get serious about data.

Here is what you find when you arrive. Legacy is not starting from zero. They have systems like Salesforce that manage customer relationships, a proprietary order management platform handling transactions, QuickBooks running the books, and Workday managing HR. The data exists. That is the good news. The problem is that almost none of it is being used systematically. Each branch operates as its own island. Reports are pulled manually, emailed as spreadsheets, and interpreted differently by different people. Nobody agrees on basic definitions. Ask two branch managers how many active customers Legacy has and you will get two different numbers. Ask finance and sales the same question and you will get two more. Decisions at Legacy are made almost entirely on gut feel and institutional memory. When two leaders disagree, the one who argues loudest in the Monday morning meeting usually wins.

Your first few weeks are spent in conversation with branch managers, regional directors, the Chief Financial Officer (CFO), the head of sales, and the VP of operations. You are not there to tell them what data can do. You are there to listen to what they need. What you're looking for are the problems they have that data can help with. We call these data use cases.

A data use case is a specific, well-scoped application of data that ties directly to one business decision or problem, rather than a general capability or goal.

That distinction is the filter for everything that follows. You set a standard for your team that you do not build things that do not solve a business problem. It does not matter how interesting the data is or how capable your team becomes. If a piece of work does not trace back to a use case like this one, it does not get built.

Nobody hands you a clean use case. What you get is a mix of complaints and requests. Reports that take too long, numbers that don't match, a branch manager who just wants a dashboard. None of that is the use case itself. The use case is the business problem sitting underneath the request, and finding it is your job, not theirs. What you hear, consistently and across every level of the organization, points to three business problems that data has a real opportunity to solve:

- **Use Case 1: Sales Performance Visibility.** Branch managers and sales teams have no reliable way to understand how their business is performing. They cannot identify which salespeople need support, which accounts are at risk, or which products are driving demand in their region. Underperforming accounts go unaddressed until they are already lost, coaching conversations happen too late to make a difference, and Legacy leaves revenue on the table every quarter. What Legacy needs is a near real-time view of branch performance that puts the right information in front of the right people without requiring a data analyst to produce it on request.

- **Use Case 2: Demand Forecasting.** Legacy's procurement team is buying on gut feel and historical habit, with no reliable view of what demand will look like next month or next quarter. Stockouts frustrate customers and drive them to competitors. Overstock ties up working capital. The result is margin erosion, customer attrition, and a procurement process that reacts to problems rather than anticipating them. What Legacy needs is the ability to predict demand by product and region with enough accuracy and lead time to make smarter procurement decisions before the problem arrives.

- **Use Case 3: Customer and Account Intelligence.** Legacy's sales reps spend significant time chasing down basic information about their accounts. When did this customer last order, what did they buy, are they trending up or down? That time is not being spent selling. At the same time, the institutional knowledge that experienced reps carry in their heads leaves with every departure. The result is inconsistent customer engagement, avoidable churn, and a sales force that is less productive than it should be. What Legacy needs is a way for anyone in the sales organization to ask a question about a customer or account and get a reliable, immediate answer, without needing to know where the data lives or how to query it.

We're going to use these three use cases to build what Caroline Carruthers and Peter Jackson, in *The Chief Data Officer's Playbook*, call an Immediate Data Strategy (IDS):[6] a scoped, near-term set of commitments designed to demonstrate value quickly and build the organizational credibility needed to pursue a longer-term transformation. We will spend Part 1 building the foundational knowledge needed to understand what it takes to deliver these use cases. In Part 2, we will develop the full data strategy that defines where Legacy is going over the next three to five years, with the IDS as its first phase. Each chapter's Legacy

---

[6] Caroline Carruthers and Peter Jackson, The Chief Data Officer's Playbook (London: Facet Publishing, 2020).

section along the way will show the specific work required in that functional area to move closer to delivering on them.

By the end of this book, you will have watched Legacy go from disconnected systems and Monday morning arguments about whose numbers are right, to a functioning data organization delivering real business value. For now, these three use cases are your north star.

The next chapter covers data governance, the function most organizations underinvest in, most often regret underinvesting in, and most struggle to build once the absence of it has already caused damage.

Two

Data Governance

Data governance is unglamorous, frequently misunderstood, and easy to deprioritize when a data organization is small.

In the early days, it seems like you can get away without it. When there are two data professionals and four source systems, informal coordination works. Definitions do not need to be written down because the team is small enough that everyone shares the same understanding. Disputes about what a number means get resolved in conversation rather than through process.

Then the team grows. Business partners multiply. More systems come online. Two executives present conflicting customer counts in the same leadership meeting, and neither of them is wrong; they are using different definitions that were never formally agreed upon. A new data product gets built on a dataset nobody officially owns, with no documented policy on who can access it or how it can be used. An AI model is deployed with no documented accountability for what happens when it produces a wrong answer.

That is when organizations discover what they should have been building from the beginning.

Ask people in a data organization what they think of governance and you will often get some version of the same answer. It's slow, bureaucratic, a team that says no, the compliance police. If you have worked somewhere with a governance program that was more about control than enablement, that reputation is understandable. But governance programs that earn that reputation are almost always programs that were built too late, in response to a crisis, by people who had to fight for every resource because nobody believed the function mattered until something went wrong.

Data governance, done well, is the infrastructure that allows everything else to scale.

It does not do the day-to-day operational work of keeping data clean and trustworthy. That is data management, which the next chapter covers. What governance does is establish who is accountable, what the rules are, and how disputes get resolved. Without it, every other investment in data quality, engineering, and AI is built on ground that can shift without warning.

What Data Governance Is

Gartner defines data governance as "the specification of decision rights and an accountability framework to ensure the appropriate behavior in the valuation, creation, consumption, and control of data and analytics."[7]

Put more plainly, data governance is the system by which an organization decides who is accountable for its data, how decisions about that data are made, what rules govern its use, and how compliance with those rules is monitored and enforced.

I think of it as a constitution for your data. It does not do the day-to-day operational work. It establishes the rules everyone else works within, defines who is responsible for what, and provides a framework for resolving disputes, just as a country's constitution shapes how its institutions operate without running those institutions itself.

Governance vs. Management

A common point of confusion in data organizations is the difference between data governance and data management.

---

[7] **Data Governance:** Gartner, "Data Governance," Gartner Glossary, gartner.com/en/information-technology/glossary/data-governance.

People use the terms interchangeably, but they are not the same thing.

Governance is oversight. Management is execution.

Data governance sets the rules. Who owns the data, who can access it, what quality standards it must meet, how long it should be retained, and what happens when something goes wrong. Data management is the operational discipline of implementing those rules. Maintaining data quality, building pipelines, running catalogs, and managing metadata.

If your governance team is doing the work of data management, something has gone wrong. And if your data management team is making governance decisions without a framework to work from, that is also a problem. The two functions need each other, but they are not the same function.

What Governance Programs Do

Most governance programs, regardless of their specific structure, focus on some combination of the following:

- Setting and enforcing policies around how data is accessed, used, secured, and shared.

- Defining quality standards: what "good" looks like for your data in terms of accuracy, completeness, consistency, and timeliness.
- Maintaining the business glossary: the organization's official, agreed-upon definitions for key business terms. What is a "customer"? What is "revenue"? What counts as a "completed transaction"? In practice, the argument over a single business term can consume an entire steering committee meeting.
- Establishing data ownership: assigning clear responsibility and authority for specific datasets to specific individuals or groups.
- Monitoring and auditing compliance with the policies the program has set.
- Managing the escalation and resolution of data quality issues, access disputes, and definitional conflicts.

The governance function is also responsible for ensuring the organization meets its regulatory obligations and for sponsoring and supporting broader data management improvement efforts across the organization.

Data Ownership: Simple in Theory, Hard in Practice

If it's everyone's responsibility, it's no one's.

Establishing data ownership is one of the first and most important steps a new governance program must take. It is also politically fraught, because ownership comes with accountability, and not everyone wants to be accountable for data that may not be in great shape.

Data ownership has two dimensions. Business ownership is about strategic value and use. Aligning data with business objectives, ensuring quality meets business needs, and making decisions about how data is acquired and used. Technical ownership is about the infrastructure layer. Designing architectures, ensuring security, and managing the systems where the data lives. Both need to exist and work together.

Data Stewardship

If data governance is the constitution, data stewardship is the day-to-day government. Stewardship is the operational layer where most governance work gets done.

A data steward is the person responsible for a specific dataset or data domain. They're the ones who understand what the data means, where it comes from, how it's supposed to be used, and what the quality standards are for it. Importantly, stewards don't have to be technical experts. A marketing manager who deeply understands the customer data his team produces can be an excellent steward for that dataset. A financial analyst who owns the revenue reporting logic is often the right steward for financial data. The question is expertise in the data itself, not expertise in the technology that stores it.

Privacy, Compliance, and Why the Stakes Are Real

Data governance is where the organization's legal exposure lives. Privacy regulations have teeth, and the enforcement environment has become more aggressive.

General Data Protection Regulation (GDPR) applies to any organization that processes the personal data of individuals in the European Union, regardless of where that organization is located. Its reach is global. Fines come in two tiers: lower-tier violations capped at €10 million or 2% of global annual turnover, whichever is higher; upper-tier violations capped at €20 million or 4% of global annual turnover. By 2025, cumulative GDPR fines exceeded €6 billion.[8] TikTok was fined €530 million in May 2025 for unlawful data transfers between the EU and China.[9] These are not hypothetical risks.

California Consumer Privacy Act (CCPA), California's consumer privacy law, applies to businesses meeting certain

---

[8] GDPR Enforcement Tracker, CMS Law.Tax, cms-lawnow.com, cumulative penalty data as reported through 2025.

[9] Irish Data Protection Commission, decision announced May 2, 2025, fining TikTok Technology Limited €530 million for GDPR transfer violations.

thresholds: more than $25 million in annual gross revenue, or annually buying, selling, or sharing the personal information of 100,000 or more consumers, or deriving 50% or more of annual revenue from selling or sharing personal information. Consumer rights include the right to know what data is collected, the right to delete, the right to correct inaccurate information, and the right to opt out of the sale or sharing of personal information.[10]

Health Insurance Portability and Accountability Act (HIPAA) governs personal health information in the United States and applies to healthcare providers, health plans, and their vendors. The Breach Notification Rule requires notification of affected individuals and regulators generally within 60 days of a PHI compromise.

Beyond these, the regulatory landscape is sprawling and accelerating. As of 2025, 20 U.S. states have passed comprehensive consumer privacy laws. Brazil's LGPD, China's PIPL, India's DPDPA, and the EU AI Act all create additional obligations. The takeaway for data leaders is to build a governance program flexible enough to adapt as the environment evolves, rather than trying to memorize every regulation.

---

[10] California Privacy Protection Agency, "CCPA/CPRA Applicability Thresholds," cppa.ca.gov.

Data Ethics: Compliance Is the Floor

You can be fully compliant with every applicable regulation and still be doing things with data that you should not be doing.

Data ethics is concerned with the moral principles that govern how data is collected, stored, analyzed, and used. Four principles appear consistently across frameworks, including the NIST AI Risk Management Framework and the OECD AI Principles:

- **Privacy** as a matter of human autonomy, not merely legal compliance. Just because you are legally allowed to collect and use certain data does not mean you should.
- **Fairness**, meaning data is used equitably and without bias. The consequences of getting this wrong are concrete. A 2019 study published in *Science* by Obermeyer et al. documented a widely used healthcare algorithm that systematically underestimated the illness severity of Black patients because it used healthcare costs as a proxy for medical need.[11] In 2024, the DOJ and CFPB took enforcement action against Fairway

---

[11] Ziad Obermeyer, Brian Powers, Christine Vogeli, and Sendhil Mullainathan, "Dissecting Racial Bias in an Algorithm Used to Manage the Health of Populations," Science 366, no. 6464 (2019): 447–53.

Independent Mortgage for redlining majority-Black neighborhoods.[12]

- **Transparency** about how data is collected, what it is used for, and how decisions made with it affect people.
- **Accountability** for what your data practices produce. When a model causes harm, someone is responsible. Governance programs that do not embed clear accountability structures for data-driven decisions leave organizations legally, reputationally, and ethically exposed.

AI Governance

No current discussion of data governance is complete without addressing AI governance, because the two are increasingly inseparable.

As organizations build and deploy predictive models, large language models, and automated decision systems, a new set of governance questions emerges. What data was this model trained on? Was that training data representative, or does it embed historical biases? Who approved this model for production use?

[12] U.S. Department of Justice and Consumer Financial Protection Bureau, "CFPB and Justice Department Take Action Against Fairway Independent Mortgage Corporation for Redlining Black Neighborhoods in Birmingham, Alabama," press release, October 15, 2024.

How do we know it is still performing as it did when we deployed it? What happens when it makes a decision that harms someone?

These are fundamentally governance questions: questions about accountability, decision rights, oversight, and risk management. The NIST AI Risk Management Framework, ISO/IEC 42001, and the EU AI Act all provide guidance for organizations seeking to extend governance into AI. Gartner predicts that by 2028, half of organizations will adopt a zero-trust posture for data governance in response to the growing volume of unverified AI-generated data.[13]

The practical implication is that your governance program needs to expand its scope. Model cards are becoming standard governance artifacts. Standardized documentation of a model's purpose, training data, performance characteristics, and known limitations. Model review and approval processes, bias testing requirements, and ongoing monitoring for model drift are becoming governance responsibilities. Build these capabilities now, before something goes wrong.

---

[13] Gartner, "Gartner Predicts by 2028, 50% of Organizations Will Adopt Zero-Trust Data Governance as Unverified AI-Generated Data Grows," press release, January 21, 2026, gartner.com.

Why Governance Programs Fail

Gartner's research has warned that a large majority of data and analytics governance initiatives will fail, citing a lack of real or manufactured crisis as the primary cause.[14] That statistic matches what I have observed.

The challenges cluster into three categories.

- **Organizational:** Without strong executive sponsorship, governance programs struggle to get traction because they require people to change behavior, and behavior change without organizational authority rarely happens at scale. Determining who owns a dataset is one thing. Getting that person to embrace the accountability that comes with it is another problem entirely. The single biggest obstacle I have encountered in implementing data governance is the lack of an executive sponsor, and the most common reason governance programs fail is that the sponsor was nominal rather than real. Present at the kickoff, absent when the political obstacles arrived. You cannot build enough momentum at the practitioner level to compensate for its absence at the top. Find the real sponsor before you do anything else.

[14] Gartner, "Gartner Predicts 80% of D&A Governance Initiatives Will Fail by 2027 Due to a Lack of a Real or Manufactured Crisis," press release, February 28, 2024, gartner.com/en/newsroom/press-releases/2024-02-28.

- **Technical:** Data quality issues make it hard to achieve governance goals on a compromised foundation. Master data management across enterprises with dozens of systems, each maintaining their own version of a customer or product record, creates complexity that governance policies alone cannot resolve.
- **Cultural:** If people in the organization do not understand why data matters or how to use it well, governance programs feel like bureaucratic overhead rather than enabling infrastructure. Building a genuine data culture is a long journey. Governance programs support that journey but cannot complete it alone.

How to Start

Starting a governance program from scratch is one of the more daunting things you can take on. Here is the approach that works:

Start with the current state. Before you can govern anything, you have to know what you have. Inventory your data assets, assess quality honestly, and evaluate your security and privacy posture against applicable regulatory requirements.

Define your objectives before you design your framework. What is the governance program supposed to accomplish? What problems are you solving? Governance programs that skip this step end up governing for governance's sake, which is exactly how you earn the reputation of being the team that says no without adding value.

You do not have to invent a governance structure from scratch, and you should not try to. Established frameworks already exist to assess where you stand and structure where you are going. The EDM Council's Data Management Capability Assessment Model (DCAM) is widely used in large enterprises, particularly in financial services, to benchmark governance maturity against a defined set of capabilities. The CMMI Data Management Maturity Model does something similar with a more granular set of process areas and maturity levels, useful when you need a detailed, staged roadmap rather than a single benchmark. COBIT, from ISACA, ties data governance into a broader IT risk and audit framework, and is the natural fit if your program has to satisfy SOX, GDPR, or a similarly compliance-heavy mandate. DAMA-DMBOK2, the reference this book draws on throughout, is itself a framework. Eleven knowledge areas cover the full scope of data management, with governance as the coordinating discipline that ties the rest together.

Start small. Gartner's concept of "minimum viable governance" is useful here. Identify the smallest set of governance controls that enables the highest-priority use case, implement those, demonstrate value, and expand from there. A governance program that works for three critical datasets is more valuable than a comprehensive framework that nobody follows.

On tools, whatever a vendor's sales deck implies, technology alone cannot solve a data governance problem. Data governance is fundamentally about organizational behavior. The right tools can help you scale and sustain a program once the organizational behavior is in place, but they cannot create it. If you are just starting, a well-maintained spreadsheet of data owners and a shared document of business definitions will outperform an unimplemented enterprise governance platform. When you are ready to invest in tooling, the 2025 Gartner Magic Quadrant for Data and Analytics Governance Platforms identified Informatica, Collibra, Alation, and IBM as leaders.[15] Atlan moved into the Leaders quadrant in 2026. Microsoft Purview is rapidly gaining ground in Microsoft-centric environments.

Further Reading

Foundational works for going deeper on this topic:

Non-Invasive Data Governance: The Path of Least Resistance and Greatest Success, by Robert S. Seiner, the classic argument for governing through existing accountability rather than new bureaucracy.

---

15 Gartner, Magic Quadrant for Data and Analytics Governance Platforms, 2025; Atlan's move into the Leaders quadrant reflects the 2026 update.

Data Governance: The Definitive Guide, by Evren Eryurek, Uri Gilad, Valliappa Lakshmanan, Anita Kibunguchy-Grant, and Jessi Ashdown, a modern, practical guide to operationalizing governance across people, process, and tools.

Data Governance: How to Design, Deploy, and Sustain an Effective Data Governance Program, by John Ladley, a complementary framework for building and sustaining a program once it exists.

Legacy Paper and Supply: Data Governance

The three use cases you identified in your first weeks at Legacy all depend on one thing Legacy does not yet have: data people can trust. The branch performance dashboard is only useful if the sales numbers it shows are accurate and consistent across branches. The demand forecasting model is only as good as the historical sales and inventory data it trains on. The customer intelligence application will produce embarrassing results if the customer records in Salesforce are duplicated, incomplete, or contradictory. Before you can build any of it, you need a governance foundation.

The first governance problem surfaces almost immediately. You ask a simple question in a meeting with the head of sales and the CFO. How many active customers does Legacy have? Sales says 1,400. Finance says 1,100. Neither of them is wrong, exactly. They are just using different definitions. Sales counts any account that has placed an order in the past 12 months. Finance counts any account with an open receivable or a transaction in the current fiscal year. Neither definition was ever written down, agreed upon, or communicated to anyone outside the respective teams. This single disagreement means Use Case 1 cannot be built until it is resolved. You cannot measure account health against a definition that two different parts of the organization do not share.

This is where governance work begins. Not with policies and frameworks, but with a conversation.

You convene a working session with representatives from sales, finance, and operations to develop a single, agreed-upon definition of an active customer. The process is more political than technical. It requires a decision-maker in the room with enough authority to break the tie when the two sides cannot agree. This is why the executive sponsor matters so much. Without someone who can say "this is the definition we are using going forward," the conversation circles indefinitely.

That single resolved conflict tells you exactly how to build the rest of the program. Find where the organization already disagrees or already trusts no one, and govern that first. You do not start by inventorying every dataset Legacy owns. You start with the handful of data domains the three use cases depend on. Customer and account data, sales transaction data, inventory and product data. For each one, you name a real owner, not a title, a specific person. The VP of Sales, who already lives in Salesforce every day, becomes the accountable owner for the customer and account domain. The controller who reconciles revenue each month becomes the owner for transaction data. Neither of them gains new headcount or a new job title. What changes is that when a data quality question comes up, there is exactly one person whose job it is to answer it.

You set up a governance working group that is deliberately small. The two domain owners, someone from IT who understands where the data lives, and you. It meets every two weeks, for thirty minutes, with one purpose: resolve the next definitional conflict or ownership gap standing in the way of a use case, and add it to the glossary. It is not a standing committee with a charter and a meeting cadence set in stone. It exists because there is work for it to do, and it will change shape as that work changes. You write a one-page charter: what this group governs, who is on it, and who has final say when it deadlocks, because the next person who has to explain why this group exists should not have to ask you.

From there, the governance priorities sequence naturally from the use cases. Use Case 1 requires clean, consistent sales and account data in Salesforce, which means establishing data ownership for the customer and sales domains and defining minimum quality standards for the fields that will power the dashboard. Use Case 2 requires reliable historical transaction and inventory data, which means establishing retention policies, documenting lineage, and setting quality thresholds for the data used to train the forecasting model. Use Case 3 requires that the customer records the AI application will query are accurate, deduplicated, and complete, because a system that confidently returns wrong information about a customer is worse than no system at all.

The governance work at Legacy will not be finished by the time the first dashboard is built. It will not be finished by the time the forecasting model goes into production. Governance is not a project with a completion date. It is an ongoing discipline that matures as the organization matures. What matters at this stage is establishing the structures that make everything else possible: ownership, definitions, standards, and accountability.

The next chapter covers data management, the operational execution layer that governance depends on to function, and the function where data quality lives or dies.

THREE

Data Management

There is a conversation I have had more times than I can count when stepping into new leadership roles, and it usually goes something like this. A business leader pulls me aside and says, "We have a lot of data problems." When I ask what they mean, they describe one of three things. They cannot find the data they need, they do not trust the data they have, or every department has built its own version of the same report, and none of them match.

All three of those problems are data management problems. And all three are solved, slowly and imperfectly, by building a strong data management function.

Data governance sets the rules. Data management is what happens when people follow them. It is the operational discipline that takes governance policies and translates them into functional data infrastructure. Clean, consistent, accessible, trustworthy data that the business can use. Governance decides what good data looks like. Management is the machinery that produces it.

What Data Management Is

DAMA International, the global professional association for data management practitioners, publishes the field's standard reference text, the Data Management Body of Knowledge, now in its second edition and commonly known as DAMA-DMBOK2. It defines data management as "the development, execution, and supervision of plans, policies, programs, and practices that deliver, control, protect, and enhance the value of data and information assets throughout their lifecycle."[16]

Notice what that definition emphasizes: delivering value. Storage, security, organization, none of that is the point. The purpose of data management is to ensure that data delivers value throughout its life, from creation to disposal.

When a data management function doesn't exist, the work does not simply disappear. Someone still has to define what an active customer means. Someone still has to reconcile the fact that the Customer Relationship Management (CRM) system and the data warehouse are showing different revenue numbers. In the absence

---

16 **Data Management:** DAMA International, DAMA-DMBOK: Data Management Body of Knowledge, 2nd ed. (Basking Ridge, NJ: Technics Publications, 2017), 15.

of a dedicated function, that work lands on whoever is closest to the problem: the data engineer who stops building pipelines to track down a quality issue or the analyst who spends half their time explaining why their numbers do not match finance's. These are among the most expensive people in the organization, doing work that a skilled data management practitioner could handle more effectively and consistently.

A data management function does not add overhead. It removes it from the people who can least afford to carry it.

Master Data Management

The same customer exists in your CRM as "Jonathan Smith," in your billing system as "J. Smith Inc.," and in your shipping system as "Smith Enterprises." Same person, three records, and nothing connecting them except someone checking by hand. That is a master data problem. The same core entity, represented inconsistently across every system that touches it.

Master data is the foundational, critical data that describes the core entities a business operates around. Customers, products, locations, suppliers, employees, etc. In most organizations without a master data management program, this data is fragmented. The CRM has one version of the customer record. The billing system has another. The shipping system has a third.

Every time someone tries to analyze customer behavior, they spend more time reconciling sources than doing analysis.

Master Data Management (MDM) is the discipline of establishing a single, consistent, authoritative version of this critical data across the organization. MDM programs are notoriously difficult to execute well. The most common failure mode is treating MDM as a technical problem when it is fundamentally a business and organizational one. Getting people to agree on what a "customer" is, and getting someone to be accountable for maintaining that definition.

Metadata Management

Metadata is data about data. What does this field represent, where did it come from, when was it last updated, who is responsible for it? Without good metadata, data is context-free. You pull a table called "customer_revenue" and you do not know whether that field represents invoiced revenue, collected revenue, or something else entirely.

Traditional metadata management was passive documentation. Active metadata is a significant evolution. Continuously collected, analyzed, and put to work, flowing from the systems that generate it into a central intelligence layer that can surface insights, trigger governance actions, and flag quality issues. In November 2025, Gartner reinstated the Magic Quadrant for Metadata

Management Solutions after a five-year hiatus, explicitly in response to AI's dependence on high-quality, well-governed metadata.[17]

Data Lineage

Imagine a dashboard that shows weekly sales performance. A VP of Sales looks at it Monday morning and something seems off. Is the data wrong? Did a source system fail? Or did sales actually decline?

Without data lineage, answering that question is a detective exercise that can take hours or days. With lineage, you can trace the data from the dashboard back through every transformation it underwent, back to the original source systems, and identify exactly where the anomaly entered the pipeline. Lineage enables faster root-cause analysis, impact assessment before changes are made, and regulatory compliance. GDPR, BCBS 239, and the EU AI Act all require some degree of data traceability.

---

[17] Gartner reinstated its Magic Quadrant for Metadata Management Solutions in November 2025 after a five-year hiatus.

Data Quality

If there is one concept in this chapter that matters more than all the others to business leaders, it is data quality. Gartner estimates that poor data quality costs organizations an average of $12.9 million per year.[18] A 2025 Precisely study found that 67% of organizations do not fully trust their own data for decision-making.[19]

Data quality is measured across dimensions that together describe what "good" data looks like: accuracy (Do values correctly represent the real-world entity?), completeness (Is all required information present?), consistency (Does data agree across systems?), timeliness (Is data current enough for its intended use?), validity (Does data conform to defined formats?), uniqueness (Is there only one record per entity?), and reasonableness (Does the data make sense in context, even if it passes every formal rule?).

That last one deserves emphasis. A transaction amount of $0.01 for a commercial real estate sale passes every validity check and is still wrong. These are the hardest issues to detect programmatically. The worst outcome is not that your business

---

[18] Gartner, Magic Quadrant for Data Quality Solutions, July 27, 2020, Melody Chien and Ankush Jain, based on a survey of 154 reference customers.

[19] Precisely, 2025 Data Integrity Trends and Insights Report (Precisely, 2025).

partner catches it. It is that nobody catches it until a decision has already been made on bad data or a model has been trained on it.

I once spent the better part of a week on a geographic analysis project cleaning city, state, and zip fields that a source system captured as free text, no dropdown, no validation, just whatever the person entering the record happened to type. I eventually counted 287 different spellings of Chihuahua, Mexico. The lesson I took from that week was not about cleaning faster. It was about where the fix belonged. Every hour spent reconciling variants was an hour spent on a symptom that a single dropdown at the point of entry would have prevented permanently. A free-text field that produces bad data once will produce the same bad data again for the next person, and the person after that. Fixing the source system is more work upfront and far less work over the life of the data, and it is worth fighting for even when you do not own that system, because you are the one who keeps paying for leaving it broken.

Modern data quality management is proactive and continuous. Automated profiling tools scan datasets against defined dimensions, alerts fire when data falls below thresholds, and ML-powered anomaly detection identifies issues that no predefined rule would have caught. Closely related is data observability, continuously monitoring pipeline health across the five pillars of freshness, volume, schema, distribution, and lineage to detect anomalies in real time.

Data as a Product

Treating data as a product rather than a byproduct of operations is an important shift in how modern data organizations think about their work. A data product is a managed, packaged data asset that is discoverable, understandable, trustworthy, and reusable. It has a defined purpose, documented schema, quality guarantees, clear ownership, and a mechanism for consumers to report problems.

The contrast is with how most organizations manage data today. Datasets exist because systems produce them, not because someone decided they should meet a defined consumer need. Quality is incidental. Documentation is sparse. When something breaks, it is often unclear who is responsible. Treating data as a product means assigning ownership, defining quality SLAs, and iterating based on what consumers need.

What AI Changes About Data Management

Gartner projects that a majority of AI projects will be abandoned due to insufficient AI-ready data. AI creates requirements that did not exist in a purely analytical environment. Tracking exactly what data was used to train a model, whether it was representative of the population the model will serve, and whether it contained biases that could produce discriminatory outputs. Feature stores ensure consistency between the variables used during training and those served at prediction time. Model lineage tracks the full provenance chain from raw data through deployment.

The most actionable implication is that if your organization is investing in AI, your data management program needs to evolve beyond traditional analytical data quality. The governance and quality disciplines in this chapter are not optional infrastructure for AI. They are prerequisites for AI that works.

Why Data Management Programs Struggle

Data quality issues accumulate and compound. Source systems change constantly without notice, and each change has the potential to silently break a downstream pipeline or corrupt a dashboard. Siloed data and systems mean relevant data often lives across multiple systems that were never designed to work together. Trust deficits may be the most damaging challenge. When business users do not trust data, they ignore it or build their own shadow datasets, which creates exactly the kind of fragmentation that data management is supposed to prevent. Rebuilding trust requires consistent, demonstrated improvement over an extended period.

Perhaps the most structurally underappreciated challenge is the funding problem that comes with doing defensive work. Lak DalleMule and Thomas Davenport, writing in the Harvard Business Review in 2017, introduced a framework that every data leader should internalize. Data activities fall into two categories. Offensive activities use data to generate value directly: building dashboards, training models, creating customer segmentation, launching AI applications. Defensive activities protect and enable that value: data quality programs, master data management, lineage documentation, governance policies, metadata management. Offensive work is visible. It produces things business partners can point to, celebrate, and attribute ROI to. Defensive work is invisible when it is working.

When data quality is excellent, nobody calls to say thank you.

When lineage is documented, nobody sends a congratulatory email. The value of defensive investment is felt most clearly in its absence, which is exactly the wrong dynamic for a budget conversation with a CFO who wants to know what they are getting for their money.[20]

This is why data management programs are chronically underfunded relative to their impact. If you go to the executive team asking for resources to build a master data management program, you will almost always be in a harder conversation than the data scientist asking for resources to build a predictive model. The model will produce a number the business can measure. Right now, every report requires an analyst to manually reconcile these

20 Lak DalleMule and Thomas H. Davenport, "What's Your Data Strategy?" Harvard Business Review, May–June 2017.

systems and make judgment calls about how they line up, judgment calls the next analyst will make differently. MDM makes that call once, so everyone downstream works from the same logic instead of re-guessing it every time. The return on the defensive investment is real and often larger in the long run. Still, it requires making visible what does not happen: the incorrect decisions that were avoided, the incidents that did not occur, and the model that trained on trustworthy data rather than corrupted data.

We will return to this challenge in Part 2's chapter on measuring the value of data, and to the offense/defense balance specifically in the chapter on building a data strategy. For now, the most important thing to understand is that the funding difficulty is not just a perception problem to be solved with better communication. It is a structural feature of what defensive work is. Understanding that going in will help you design a data management program to generate visible wins alongside the invisible foundational work, connecting every quality improvement to a business outcome someone upstairs cares about.

How to Build a Data Management Function

Start with business value. A quality program that governs ten critical datasets well is worth more than one that nominally covers everything and governs nothing. Build quality into processes rather than retrofitting it; it is cheaper to prevent problems at the point of creation than to remediate them later. Build the governance foundation first, since data management cannot succeed without clear ownership, defined policies, and agreed-upon definitions.

On tooling for data quality, Informatica and Ataccama lead the Gartner quadrant. For MDM, Informatica, Stibo Systems, SAP, and Reltio are well-established. For metadata management and catalogs, Atlan, Collibra, Alation, and IBM lead. For data observability, Monte Carlo is the most widely deployed, alongside Acceldata, Soda, and Anomalo. Platform-native options from Databricks, Snowflake, and Microsoft Fabric are embedding many of these capabilities directly into the storage layer.

The same caution applies everywhere: a data quality tool configured against the wrong standards produces meaningless metrics. Every tool investment should be preceded by a clear understanding of what organizational behavior it is meant to support.

Further Reading

Foundational works for going deeper on this topic:

DAMA-DMBOK: Data Management Body of Knowledge, 2nd ed., by DAMA International, the definitive reference for master data, metadata, and data quality practice.

Master Data Management, by David Loshin, the standard reference for MDM programs, with a clear-eyed focus on the organizational politics as much as the technical design.

Executing Data Quality Projects, by Danette McGilvray, a structured, practical methodology for running a data quality program end to end.

Legacy Paper and Supply: Data Management

The governance work you began in the previous chapter established the rules. Now comes the harder part, determining whether the data in Legacy's systems is sufficient to build on.

The answer, when you start looking, is that it is better than you feared and worse than you hoped.

Salesforce has customer records going back several years, but they are riddled with problems. Duplicate accounts are common. The same customer appears under slightly different names across branches because each branch entered records independently, with no standardization. Contact information is inconsistent. Account status fields are unreliable because, until you defined "active customer" in the governance chapter, different reps were updating the field according to their own judgment.

QuickBooks tells a similar story on the financial side. The chart of accounts has been modified over the years in ways that make historical comparisons difficult. Some transactions are inconsistently categorized across branches, which means the financial data that will feed Use Case 2 will require significant remediation before it is usable.

The order management platform is the cleanest of the three. Transactions are recorded systematically and consistently, the fields are populated, and the history is relatively complete. This is the data that will power Use Case 1 most directly, and it is encouraging that the foundation is solid.

This profiling exercise is where data management work always begins. Understand what you have before you decide what to fix. Salesforce shows roughly 1,800 customer records against an active base that sales and finance already agreed, in the governance chapter, sits somewhere between 1,100 and 1,400 depending on the definition applied. That gap, as much as a third of the records in the system, is duplicates, stale accounts, and departed customers nobody archived. That number is your baseline. Six months from now, you will measure progress against it.

Deduplication itself is not a fully automatable problem, and treating it like one is how these efforts stall. You start with fuzzy matching on name, phone number, and billing address to surface likely duplicate pairs, which handles the obvious cases, the same company entered as "Smith Hardware" in one branch and "Smith Hardware Inc." in another. What the algorithm cannot resolve, such as two accounts that might be the same customer or might be two locations of a franchise, gets routed to a person for a judgment call. That person is the VP of Sales, the domain owner you named in the governance chapter, because ambiguous merges are exactly the kind of decision an owner exists to make. You are not asking him to do data entry. You are asking his team to spend an hour a week for a few weeks resolving the fifty or so cases the algorithm could not.

With the profile complete, the remediation priorities sequence from the use cases. Use Case 1 requires deduplicating the Salesforce customer records and establishing minimum quality standards for the fields that will appear in the branch dashboard. Use Case 2 requires reliable historical transaction data going back at least two to three years, with lineage documented so that when a model produces a prediction, you can trace it back to the data it was trained on. Use Case 3 requires that the customer records the AI application will query are accurate, deduplicated, and complete. A system that confidently tells a sales rep that a customer last ordered six months ago, when the actual last order was last week, destroys trust faster than any technical failure would. The quality bar for data surfacing directly to end users via a conversational interface is higher than for data feeding a dashboard, because a confident wrong answer from an AI assistant gives them nothing but misinformation.

None of this is quick work. Data management maturity is measured in years, not months. But organizations that start with what matters most and build trust through demonstrated improvement do reach a point where the business can rely on its data. At Legacy, you are now closer to that point than you were when you arrived.

The next chapter covers data architecture, the structural blueprint that determines how your data is organized, how it flows through the organization, and whether the infrastructure you build today can support the capabilities you will need tomorrow.

FOUR

Data Architecture

Every modern building that has ever been constructed started as a blueprint, because trying to build something complex without a plan is how you end up with load-bearing walls in the wrong places, plumbing that does not connect, and a structure that cannot be modified without tearing half of it down.

Data organizations make this mistake constantly. They build first and plan later. A dataset gets created for one application. Another gets created for a second. A third team stands up their own data lake because the first two do not give them what they need. Over time, the organization accumulates a tangle of systems that overlap in some places and conflict in others, with data flowing through unofficial pathways that nobody fully understands and that break whenever something changes upstream. Then someone in the executive suite asks for a single view of the customer, and the data team has to explain why it will take two years.

Data architecture is the discipline that prevents this. It is the practice of designing your data environment intentionally, before you build it, in a way that serves where your business is going rather than just where it is today. Data modeling is the primary tool architects use to make those designs concrete, communicable, and buildable.

Together, architecture and modeling represent the intellectual foundation of everything downstream. Without them, your data engineering team is building pipelines to nowhere. Your analytics team is querying data they do not fully understand. Your governance team is trying to govern systems that are irrelevant to your use cases.

What Data Architecture Is

DAMA-DMBOK2 describes the goal of data architecture as identifying the data needs of the enterprise, designing and maintaining the master blueprints to meet those needs, and using those blueprints to guide data integration, control data assets, and align data investments with business strategy. The specific outputs are three: models, definitions, and data flows.[21]

---

[21] **Data Architecture:** DAMA International, DAMA-DMBOK: Data Management Body of Knowledge, 2nd ed. (Basking Ridge, NJ: Technics Publications, 2017), chapter 4.

Data architects sit at a specific intersection. They have to understand the business requirements well enough to know what the data environment needs to support. They have to then understand technology well enough to know what is buildable. And they have to bridge the two, translating business strategy into data requirements and translating data capabilities into business outcomes. Architecture is also the organization's institutional memory for data. Without it, every new project starts from scratch. With it, new initiatives build on a common foundation, and the organization accumulates capability over time rather than reinventing the wheel on every engagement.

Data architecture is not a one-time deliverable.

Organizations that treat it as a project with an end date end up with architecture that deteriorates. Systems gradually become more complex and inflexible. Technical debt accumulates invisibly until it surfaces as failures, slow delivery, and escalating costs. A mature architecture program balances two ongoing activities, maintaining the existing environment and innovating to support new capabilities.

What Data Modeling Is

Data modeling is the process of discovering, analyzing, and scoping data requirements, then representing and communicating those requirements in a precise, visual form called a data model. It creates a common language between business stakeholders and technical teams. It documents business rules in a rigorous form, making requirements explicit rather than leaving them in someone's head. And it identifies problems before they become expensive, catching inconsistencies during the design phase when they are cheap to fix rather than after implementation when they are not.

Data models exist at three levels of abstraction, each serving a different audience.

The **conceptual model** captures the high-level business requirements, the major entities (Customer, Order, Product, Branch) and their relationships. It uses business language, stays deliberately abstract, and in theory is designed to be read and validated by business stakeholders before any technical design work begins.

The **logical model** refines the conceptual model into a detailed technical representation, adding attributes, keys, data types, and constraints. It remains independent of any specific database platform, describing what the data should look like rather than how it will be implemented.

The **physical model** represents the actual implementation in a specific system, adapting the logical model to the chosen technology by incorporating indexes, partitioning strategies, and storage-optimization choices. The Snowflake and Oracle versions of the same logical model will look different.

Data Flow Diagrams

Where a data model describes what your data looks like, a data flow diagram describes how it moves. It maps the actual path data takes. It shows which system it originates in, which processes touch and transform it along the way, where it comes to rest, and which other systems or people consume it downstream.

The notation is simple by design: external entities (the sources and destinations outside the system being mapped, such as a customer, a payment processor, or a regional office); processes (the points where data gets transformed, validated, or combined); data stores (where it comes to rest between processes); and data flows (the arrows connecting all of it, each one labeled with what is actually moving along it). Most useful diagrams start at a high level, a single page showing how data moves between major systems, before anyone drills into the detail of any one process.

This is a different artifact than the data lineage discussed in the previous chapter, and the distinction is worth holding onto. A data flow diagram is drawn proactively, during design, to show how data is supposed to move. Lineage is typically captured automatically, after the fact, to trace how one specific piece of data got somewhere. You design with one and audit with the other, and a healthy architecture practice needs both.

Data Architecture in the Age of AI

Data architecture has always had to evolve as new computing paradigms emerged. The shift to AI requires a set of architectural components that most traditional architecture programs have not yet incorporated. Three of them matter most for you to understand conceptually.

Feature stores are centralized repositories of the derived variables that machine learning models use as inputs. Without a feature store, the features used to train a model may be calculated differently than the features served to that model at prediction time, quietly undermining model performance. A feature store ensures consistency between training and serving and enables feature reuse across models and teams.

Vector databases are storage systems designed for embeddings, numerical representations of content (a document, a product description, an image) that capture semantic meaning in a way that allows similarity to be computed mathematically. When you search a knowledge base and get results that are conceptually related to your query even though they share no exact keywords, that is vector search operating on embeddings. Vector databases are now a standard architectural component for any organization building AI applications that need to find semantically similar content.

Retrieval-Augmented Generation (RAG) is an architectural pattern for grounding AI language model outputs in your organization's specific data. When a user asks a question, the system first retrieves relevant documents from a knowledge base using vector search, then passes those retrieved pieces as context to the language model, which generates an answer grounded in that specific, current, trusted content. RAG is the dominant pattern for enterprise AI assistants and internal knowledge bases because it dramatically reduces hallucination and allows the AI to reason over your data without expensive model retraining.

The leadership-level takeaway is that the data architecture your organization builds today is the substrate on which your AI investments will run tomorrow. Organizations that invest in clean data, clear lineage, governed metadata, and consistent models are also building AI-ready infrastructure. Organizations that defer that investment will find themselves unable to use AI effectively even when they invest in it, because the data will not be trustworthy enough to train on or reliable enough to serve from.

Common Challenges

Balancing governance with innovation is the central tension. Too much governance and the architecture function becomes a bottleneck. Every new initiative waits weeks for a review that produces a document nobody reads. Too little governance and the estate deteriorates through architectural drift, accumulating inconsistencies that make future change exponentially more difficult.

Keeping architecture current is a continuous effort most organizations underinvest in. Architecture that accurately describes the system as it was designed three years ago but no longer reflects how it operates is worse than no architecture at all, because it creates false confidence in decisions based on inaccurate maps.

How to Build an Architecture Practice

Start with business capabilities, not technical components. An architecture roadmap that cannot be traced to specific business outcomes will lose executive support. Design for change, not just for today. Every architectural decision is a constraint on future flexibility, and decisions that are expensive to reverse deserve more scrutiny than decisions that are cheap to undo. Treat architecture governance as an enabling function rather than a policing function. Reference architectures and approved patterns that make the right choice the easy choice will produce better adoption than review boards that say no without offering alternatives.

On tooling, traditional enterprise modeling platforms like erwin, ER/Studio, and SAP PowerDesigner serve large, regulated environments with strict compliance requirements. For most teams building on cloud platforms today, SqlDBM, dbdiagram.io, and Lucidchart cover conceptual through physical modeling needs. Data build tool (dbt) deserves special mention. Though its primary identity is as a transformation tool, its model definitions, tests, and documentation constitute a full modeling practice for the analytics layer in cloud-native stacks. A well-maintained dbdiagram.io schema the team actually uses is worth more than an enterprise-licensed platform that nobody opens.

Further Reading

Foundational works for going deeper on this topic:

Data Modeling Made Simple, by Steve Hoberman, the standard introduction to reading and building data models, from someone who has taught it to thousands.

Building the Data Lakehouse, by Bill Inmon, Mary Levins, and Ranjeet Srivastava, from the person credited as the father of the data warehouse, on where architecture is heading next.

The Data Warehouse Toolkit, by Ralph Kimball, the enduring reference for dimensional modeling; most BI teams are still using ideas from this book, knowingly or not.

Legacy Paper and Supply: Data Architecture

The governance work established who owns the data and what it means. The data management work established that the data in Legacy's systems is usable, with remediation underway. Now comes the question that determines whether any of the three use cases can be built. How should that data be structured and organized to support the analytical, predictive, and AI workloads you plan?

Use Case 1, sales performance visibility, is fundamentally a reporting and analytics problem. It needs a clean, queryable view of sales transactions, customer accounts, salespeople, and branches, organized to make it fast to slice and dice by region, time period, product category, and account. This is the textbook use case for dimensional modeling. A star schema built around a central sales fact table, with dimension tables for Customer, Salesperson, Product, Branch, and Date, will answer the first generation of branch-level questions and serve as the foundation for the forecasting work in Use Case 2.

Use Case 2, demand forecasting, requires historical transaction data at a granular level, ideally daily or weekly order data by product and branch going back several years, along with inventory data, stock levels, reorder points, and lead times. The architecture needs to preserve that historical granularity rather than aggregating it away, and it needs to maintain lineage between the raw source data and the training datasets the model will consume.

If the model is retrained, the architecture needs to support that cleanly without corrupting the historical record.

Use Case 3, customer and account intelligence, introduces a third architectural requirement: the data must be accessible via a natural language interface. That means it needs to be well-documented, consistently structured, and semantically clear enough for a large language model to reason about accurately. A customer record with ambiguous fields, inconsistent naming conventions, or missing values will produce unreliable responses from an AI assistant. The architecture for Use Case 3 is as much about data quality and documentation as it is about structure.

With those requirements in hand, the architectural design for Legacy becomes clear. The conceptual model centers on six core entities: Customer, Order, Product, Branch, Salesperson, and Supplier. Customers place orders. Orders contain products. Salespeople process orders. Salespeople belong to branches. Products are sourced from suppliers. That conceptual model gets translated into a logical model with attributes and keys, and then into a physical model implemented in a cloud data warehouse.

Document what you build. The conceptual model is a governance artifact that will pay dividends for years, establishing the vocabulary, clarifying the business rules, and giving every future architect and engineer a map to work from. Every good architectural decision made today makes the next decision easier. Every shortcut taken today becomes debt that constrains tomorrow's options.

The next chapter covers data engineering, the function that takes the architectural blueprint and builds the pipelines, platforms, and infrastructure that move data from where it is created to where it creates value.

FIVE

Data Engineering

Every number a business leader trusts has already traveled a long way to get there. Start with something small. A customer places an order online through a company's web application. That transaction gets written to the operational database powering the site, structured for speed, not for analysis. Later that evening, an extraction job copies it into the data lake, alongside millions of other rows nobody will look at individually. From there, a transformation step runs, joining that order to the customer's account, converting the timestamp to the company's reporting time zone, categorizing the product into the right line of business, and calculating the margin. The result gets written to a new table, one built to answer the kinds of questions the business asks. Only then can a dashboard query it, or a forecasting model include it in tomorrow's training run.

That is the data engineering work, repeated continuously, for every order, every customer interaction, every inventory update, all day, every day. Extraction, transformation, storage, and the orchestration that keeps all of it running in the right order. Data engineering is the discipline of building and operating that entire path, so that by the time a number reaches a dashboard or a model, it is accurate, current, and in a useful form.

What Data Engineering Is

Data engineers build and maintain the infrastructure that makes data accessible, reliable, and fit for use.

> *Their work is largely invisible when it is functioning correctly and highly visible when it is not.*

Core responsibilities include extracting data from a range of sources (databases, APIs, files, event streams, third-party services), transforming it by cleaning and standardizing it, loading it into appropriate storage systems, and building and maintaining the automated pipelines that keep data flowing between systems. Data engineers also partner with governance teams to implement access, security, and compliance policies.

The clearest way to see why data engineering matters is to trace what happens without it. Analysts spend their time chasing data rather than analyzing it. Models train on corrupted inputs and produce untrustworthy outputs. Dashboards time out and executives stop using them.

The investment is not optional. It is foundational.

Cloud and Storage Infrastructure

Before the cloud, building a data warehouse meant procuring hardware, licensing expensive software, and managing physical infrastructure. The costs were high, the lead times were long, and the capacity was fixed. Cloud computing changed all of that. Storage became effectively unlimited and priced by consumption. Compute became elastic. The barrier to standing up a sophisticated data platform dropped dramatically.

The three dominant cloud providers each offer a comprehensive suite of data engineering services. AWS is the market share leader, with S3, Redshift, Glue, and managed services for Kafka, Spark, and Airflow. Azure is the leading choice for enterprises already in the Microsoft ecosystem, anchored by Azure Data Lake Storage, Microsoft Fabric, Azure Data Factory, and Azure Databricks. GCP is the natural home for organizations prioritizing AI and machine learning, with BigQuery as its flagship analytics service.

Platform decisions are now strategic. Choosing AWS, Azure, or GCP is a long-term commitment with real implications for costs, capabilities, and vendor dependencies. Cloud economics also require active management. Spending scales with usage in ways that are easy to underestimate, and unoptimized pipelines and idle compute routinely produce surprise costs.

Where all this data lives comes down to four storage paradigms, and the differences matter operationally, not just academically.

Relational databases are built for transactions. One order, one customer update, one inventory adjustment at a time, read and written quickly and reliably. They are the system of record for operational applications, the database behind the website taking that order from the chapter's opening. They are the wrong tool for analysis. Asking a transactional database to scan millions of historical orders to calculate a trend competes directly with the live traffic it exists to serve.

Data warehouses solve that problem by separating analytical work from operational work. Data gets extracted from the transactional systems, restructured for fast scanning across large volumes, and loaded into a platform purpose-built for that kind of query; Snowflake, Redshift, and BigQuery are the most common examples. The tradeoff is that the structure has to be defined before the data arrives. If the data does not fit the schema, it does not go in.

Data lakes remove that constraint. They accept data in any format, structured, semi-structured, or completely unstructured, at a fraction of the storage cost, and defer the question of structure until someone queries it. That flexibility is also the risk. A data lake with no governance discipline around it becomes what practitioners call a data swamp, a growing pile of undocumented files that nobody can use with confidence, because nobody can say what is actually in them.

Data lakehouses are the attempt to get both. Modern table formats layered on top of lake storage add the reliability guarantees warehouses provide, consistent transactions, enforced structure where you want it, without giving up the lake's flexibility or cost advantage. That combination is why the lakehouse has become the dominant architecture for new data platform builds rather than a niche alternative to the other three.

The Medallion Architecture

The medallion architecture, popularized by Databricks and now broadly adopted across Microsoft Fabric and the wider lakehouse ecosystem, organizes data into three progressively refined layers.[22]

The **bronze** layer is raw. Data lands here exactly as received from source systems, unchanged and unvalidated. This layer is append-only and serves as the permanent record of what was ingested,

---

[22] **Data Engineering:** The medallion architecture (bronze/silver/gold) is a Databricks-popularized pattern; see Databricks, "What Is a Medallion Architecture?" databricks.com.

enabling reprocessing if a downstream transformation turns out to have been wrong.

The **silver** layer is cleaned and conformed. Bronze data is validated, deduplicated, standardized, and enriched before being written here. Silver tables represent the organization's canonical view of each entity. A customer is a customer, with consistent formatting and resolved duplicates. This is where data quality rules are applied and enforced.

The **gold** layer is business-ready. Silver data is aggregated, modeled, and prepared for downstream consumption by analytics, BI, and data science. Gold tables answer specific business questions: sales by region and month, customer lifetime value by segment, inventory turns by product category. These power dashboards and fuel most business decisions.

The benefit for data leaders is a clean separation of concerns. Raw ingestion, data quality and governance, and business logic each have their own layer with their own ownership and access controls.

Data Movement Patterns

ETL (Extract, Transform, Load) was the dominant pattern for decades. Transform data before loading it into the target system, born of an era when storage was expensive.

ELT (Extract, Load, Transform) became the modern default with the rise of cloud warehouses. Load data raw first, then transform it using the warehouse's own processing power. Raw data is preserved for reprocessing and transformations are version-controlled and testable.

Reverse ETL pushes modeled data back out from the warehouse into operational systems. It makes the analytics layer actionable by surfacing enriched data to the systems where salespeople and marketers work.

Data also moves in two rhythms. Batch processing moves data in large chunks at scheduled intervals, simpler, less expensive, and adequate for most analytical use cases. Streaming processing ingests and processes data continuously as it is generated, essential when decisions cannot wait for a nightly batch.

Pipeline Orchestration

A data pipeline is a sequence of steps, each of which depends on the previous one completing successfully, running on different schedules, and having upstream dependencies on other pipelines. Pipeline orchestration is the discipline of scheduling, monitoring, and managing these dependencies reliably. Without it, data teams discover broken pipelines when an analyst notices a missing report rather than when the failure occurred.

Apache Airflow is the industry standard, used by tens of thousands of organizations; Airflow 3.0, released in April 2025, introduced DAG versioning and event-driven scheduling.[23] Dagster takes an asset-oriented approach, tracking data assets and their lineage. Prefect is Python-first and designed for teams that want flexibility without the infrastructure complexity of Airflow. Platform-native options from Databricks, Snowflake, and Microsoft Fabric are increasingly popular for teams already standardized on those platforms.

Big Data Technologies

Three technologies from the early 2010s profoundly shaped data engineering. Apache Hadoop was the original open-source big data platform, built around distributed file storage and parallel processing. It is no longer recommended for new builds. Cloud object storage has replaced HDFS and Spark has replaced MapReduce. Hadoop remains in production at many large enterprises in financial services, healthcare, and government, and belongs in any data engineering curriculum as foundational history.

Apache Spark is the dominant distributed computing framework for modern data engineering, processing data in memory rather

[23] Apache Software Foundation, Apache Airflow 3.0 release notes, April 2025, airflow.apache.org.

than on disk to deliver dramatically faster, iterative workloads. It powers most of Databricks' platform and is deeply embedded in managed cloud services across AWS, GCP, and Azure.

Apache Kafka is the dominant streaming platform for real-time data transport, retained across topics so consumers can replay historical data. Its companion for stateful stream processing is Apache Flink, which handles filtering, aggregating, and joining streams in real time. The Kafka-plus-Flink combination has become the canonical streaming architecture.

Data Engineering and AI

AI has significantly expanded the scope of data engineering. Data engineers now build feature pipelines that compute and store the derived variables machine learning models use as inputs, ensuring training and serving features are computed identically. They build embedding pipelines that transform documents and unstructured content into vector representations for semantic search and retrieval-augmented generation. And they maintain the data quality and lineage traceability that AI governance requires. The EU AI Act and GDPR increasingly require organizations to demonstrate the provenance of data used to train their models. Gartner's research has consistently found that poor data quality is a leading cause of AI initiative failures.

Common Challenges

Data quality issues are the most persistent. The dbt Labs *2024 State of Analytics Engineering* report found that 57% of practitioners cite poor data quality as their top challenge, up from 41% two years earlier.[24] When consumers lose trust in data and stop using it, the data team loses the organizational credibility it needs to drive adoption of better practices.

Tool sprawl is a growing concern for organizations that have enthusiastically adopted the modern data stack. A stack of 12 best-of-breed tools creates a maintenance burden that small teams struggle to absorb, which is the primary driver behind consolidation.

Cost management has emerged as a board-level concern. Unoptimized pipelines and idle compute routinely produce surprise bills. Talent acquisition is difficult; the combination of Python, SQL, distributed systems, cloud infrastructure, and domain knowledge required of strong data engineers is rare.

How to Build a Data Engineering Function

Build for reliability first. Every pipeline failure erodes trust, and rebuilding trust with analytics consumers is far harder than

[24] dbt Labs, 2024 State of Analytics Engineering Report (dbt Labs, 2024).

building it in the first place. Invest in automated testing, monitoring, and alerting before investing in new capabilities.

Design for observability from the start. Define what healthy looks like for each dataset: freshness, volume, schema, distribution. It is far easier to build observability into a pipeline during design than to retrofit it after a failure.

Adopt DataOps practices. Treat data pipelines like software, version-control them, test them before deploying changes, and use CI/CD to automate deployment.

Further Reading

Foundational works for going deeper on this topic:

Fundamentals of Data Engineering, by Joe Reis and Matt Housley, the current standard for the modern data engineering lifecycle, from ingestion through serving.

Designing Data-Intensive Applications, by Martin Kleppmann, denser and more systems-level, essential once you're making real infrastructure tradeoffs.

Legacy Paper and Supply: Data Engineering

The governance policies are in place. The data has been profiled and remediation is underway. The architecture has been designed. Now comes the work that makes everything real, building the pipelines that move data from Legacy's source systems into a structure where it can be used.

Salesforce holds customer and account data. The order management platform holds transaction history. QuickBooks holds financial data. Workday holds employee and salesperson records. The engineering work involves connecting these systems, cleaning their outputs, and organizing them into a platform that can reliably serve all three use cases.

The first decision is platform selection. Snowflake, BigQuery, Redshift, and Microsoft Fabric are all capable. At Legacy's scale and maturity, the differences between them matter less than picking one and committing to it. Indecision here is more expensive than an imperfect choice.

Once the platform is selected, Fivetran or Airbyte can connect to Salesforce, QuickBooks, and Workday with minimal custom development and begin landing raw data into the bronze layer within days. The goal at this stage is not perfection. It is getting raw data flowing reliably so the transformation work can begin.

The silver layer applies the quality rules established during data management work, deduplicating customer records, standardizing product category codes, resolving the account status inconsistencies, and applying the agreed-upon definition of an active customer. By the time data reaches silver, it reflects the single version of truth that leadership agreed to.

The gold layer is where the use cases come to life. For Use Case 1, the first gold tables are sales performance by salesperson and branch, account health indicators by customer, and product demand by region. These will power the first branch dashboard. For Use Case 2, the gold layer preserves transaction history at the daily order level, by product and branch, along with inventory positions, at the granularity required by the forecasting model. For Use Case 3, the gold layer produces a clean, well-documented customer and account record that a large language model can reason about reliably.

Before any of this goes to production, define completeness thresholds, freshness windows, and row count expectations for each gold table. Set up alerts so the engineering team knows when something breaks before a branch manager opens a dashboard and finds a number that does not look right. The trust that Use Case 1 depends on is fragile in the early days, and a single undetected data incident will set the program back much further than the technical failure itself.

The streaming capabilities, feature stores, and advanced orchestration that a more mature organization would have will come later. What Legacy needs right now is a foundation that is reliable, monitored, connected to the right sources, and built around the specific outputs the three use cases require. Everything else follows from getting that right.

The next chapter covers business intelligence and analytics, the function that takes the data engineering team's output and turns it into the information, insights, and decisions that justify everything the data organization has built.

SIX

Business Intelligence and Analytics

All modern organizations create data. What separates the ones that benefit from it is the ability to turn raw data into decisions that change how the business operates.

That gap, between the data that exists and the decisions it informs, is the problem that business intelligence and analytics exist to close. And it is a harder problem than it looks. The infrastructure challenges are real. You need clean data, reliable pipelines, a governed semantic layer, and tools people can use. But even when all of that is in place, organizations routinely find that the dashboards are built, the reports are sent, and the insight never makes it into the room where the decision happens.

Business intelligence and analytics is the function closest to the business. Where data engineering builds the infrastructure and data management ensures the quality, BI and analytics ask, "What does this data mean for how we run the company?" It is, for many data leaders, the most visible and most politically consequential function in the data organization. When it works well, executives trust data and use it. When it does not, they revert to gut feel and the data organization loses the credibility it needs to do anything else.

BI vs. Analytics: Why the Distinction Matters

These two terms get used interchangeably, but the relationship between them is not two competing categories. It is a hierarchy. Business intelligence is the descriptive layer of a much larger discipline. Analytics is that larger discipline in full.

Business intelligence answers the most basic question. What happened? It is retrospective by nature. BI tells you where revenue came from last quarter, which products are moving, which branches are performing above plan. The outputs are dashboards, reports, and structured summaries designed for broad consumption.

Analytics starts at that same question, and then keeps going. Why did it happen, what is likely to happen next, what should we do about it? The outputs shift from reports toward insights, recommendations, and models.

Think of it this way. A car dashboard is BI, a continuous, real-time view of the system's current state, always available, designed for the person making decisions. A mechanic running diagnostics after the engine light comes on is doing the deeper analytics work: a specific question, a structured investigation, a conclusion about cause. Both are necessary, and the mistake is confusing which tool to reach for when.

Most organizations are significantly more mature at BI than at analytics. Getting descriptive reporting right, the part BI already handles, is the prerequisite for doing the diagnostic, predictive, and prescriptive work analytics adds on top of it.

The Four Types of Analytics

The field creates progressively more value across four levels, each building on the one before.

Descriptive analytics is the layer BI occupies. What happened? Sales reports, traffic summaries, financial statements. Most organizations spend most of their analytics capacity here, and without getting this right, nothing else is possible.

Diagnostic analytics asks: Why did it happen? It moves from description to explanation through root-cause analysis, correlation, and segmentation. This is where analytical skill begins to create real differentiation.

Predictive analytics asks: What is likely to happen? Statistical models and machine learning forecast future outcomes. Which customers are most likely to churn? Which equipment is likely to fail? Predictive analytics produces likelihoods, not certainties, and managing that distinction with business stakeholders is an important communication challenge in the function.

Prescriptive analytics asks: What should we do about it? It combines prediction with optimization to recommend specific actions. Not just which customers are likely to churn, but which retention offer is most likely to keep each of them, ranked by expected return.

Most organizations cluster at descriptive and diagnostic. Moving up the curve requires better data quality, stronger governance, deeper statistical capability, and a culture willing to act on model outputs. Technology is the least of it.

Goodhart's Law and Why KPIs Fail

No concept is more practically important for you to understand when working with metrics than Goodhart's Law: when a measure becomes a target, it ceases to be a good measure.

The insight is straightforward. Whenever an organization places significant pressure on a specific metric, people begin optimizing for that metric in ways that undermine what it was originally designed to track.

The airline industry offers a vivid illustration. D0, pronounced "dee zero," measures the percentage of flights that push back from the gate at or before their scheduled departure time. The intent is sensible, on-time departures correlate with on-time arrivals, which correlate with passenger satisfaction and revenue. But when D0 became a central management target at several major carriers, gate agents began closing jet bridges early to protect the number, leaving connecting passengers stranded on the jetway. Aircraft pushed back on time and then sat waiting for a gate. Flight crews learned the metric required them to push back, not to actually depart. This dynamic has drawn public criticism from pilots, passengers, and aviation trade press at more than one major carrier for years, and some have since adjusted their scheduling approach to rebalance against customer outcomes.[25]

There is a second problem with D0 that is subtler and more damaging. The metric only measures whether a flight is delayed, not how long. Once a flight is late, the incentive structure collapses; everyone was trained to care about D0, so there is no accountability structure in place to minimize a delay once it has

---

[25] Reported extensively in aviation trade press across multiple years, including Gary Leff's "View From the Wing" and other industry coverage, criticizing the D0 metric for incentivizing early gate closures at the expense of customer experience; American has since begun de-peaking hub schedules and adding block time.

started, recover the aircraft quickly, or prevent the cascade that one late departure sends through the rest of the day's schedule.

Good metric design accounts for what happens when the target is missed, not only what happens when it is hit.

The pattern repeats everywhere. A call center measuring average handle time produces agents who end calls before problems are solved. A data team measured on dashboards built generates hundreds of dashboards nobody uses. An analytics function measured on report volume produces reports nobody acts on.

The antidote is not to stop measuring. It is to measure multiple things simultaneously so that no single number can tell a misleading story on its own, and together they come closer to the whole picture. Before a metric goes live, especially one a business leader is excited about, it is worth asking what it could reward that nobody intended. What happens when the target is missed, what gets quietly sacrificed to hit it, what the number cannot see at all. The more pressure attached to improving that metric, bonuses tied to it, public reporting, an executive who asks about it every week, the stronger that phenomenon becomes. A metric nobody is watching closely rarely gets gamed. One with real consequences attached almost always eventually will be. That is not a one-time check. A metric that was honest last year can be gamed this year even without anyone making a conscious decision to do so. The habit is to stay alert to that possibility by default.

The Last-Mile Problem

There is a concept in analytics that should be more widely understood in data leadership: the last-mile problem.

The analogy comes from logistics, where the last mile, getting a package from the distribution hub to the customer's door, is often the most expensive and difficult part of the entire delivery chain. In analytics, the last-mile problem describes a remarkably similar phenomenon. Organizations invest heavily in data infrastructure, governance, modeling, and visualization, and then the insight fails to make it into the room where the decision happens. The analysis was correct. The dashboard was built. The report was distributed. And nothing changed.

Brent Dykes, who named and popularized this concept,[26] identifies the last mile as the phase between insight delivery and action, and argues it is where most analytics projects fail. The failure modes are familiar: insights delivered to the wrong audience at the wrong time; insights buried in a report nobody reads; insights presented in technical language the decision-maker cannot interpret; insights delivered without a clear recommendation about what to do; or insights delivered to someone who lacks the authority or incentive to act on them.

[26] Brent Dykes, Effective Data Storytelling: How to Drive Change with Data, Narrative, and Visuals (Hoboken, NJ: Wiley, 2019).

The practical implication for data leaders is significant. When an analytics project is scoped, the last-mile question should be asked before the first query is run. Who specifically will act on this, what exactly will they do differently, and what does success look like in terms of a changed decision? Working backward from action to analysis, rather than forward from data to output, is the discipline that separates analytics organizations that influence the business from those that merely inform it.

Communicating Data Visually

The last-mile problem is partly a communication problem, and a significant part of that communication happens visually. Dashboards, charts, and slide decks are where data analysis meets the people who need to act on it. Most data professionals have strong analytical skills and weak visual communication skills. The gap between those two is where insight dies.

Cole Nussbaumer Knaflic's *Storytelling with Data* (2015) remains the most practical guide to this problem. Her central argument is that most charts produced by data teams contain far more information than the audience can process, and the signal that matters gets buried in visual noise.[27] The discipline she teaches is

---

[27] **Business Intelligence and Analytics:** Cole Nussbaumer Knaflic, Storytelling with Data: A Data Visualization Guide for Business Professionals (Hoboken, NJ: Wiley, 2015).

ruthless simplification: choose the right chart for what you are trying to show, eliminate every element that does not serve the insight, and make the conclusion visible before the reader has to search for it.

- **Choose the chart that serves the question, not the default:** Bar charts compare. Line charts show change over time. Scatter plots reveal relationships. Pie charts are almost always the wrong choice because human visual perception is poor at comparing angles and arc lengths. A data leader who reviews a quarterly business review deck before it goes to the executive team and asks, "Does this chart answer the question it is supposed to answer?" will catch most of the problems before they land in the room.
- **Make the insight explicit:** Most charts produced by analysts are descriptive: here is what the data shows. Most charts that change decisions are prescriptive: here is what you should do about it, and here is the evidence. Titles like "Q3 Sales by Region" describe. Titles like "Northeast Underperforming Target by 18% for Second Consecutive Quarter" conclude. The second version does the reader's interpretive work for them, which is the point. A busy executive reading a 12-slide deck in twenty minutes will remember the conclusion in the title long after they've forgotten the chart below it.
- **Reduce cognitive load before adding polish:** The instinct to make charts look more polished, with

gradients, 3D effects, background colors, and decorative elements, almost always makes them harder to read. Every visual element the reader's eye must process costs attention that should be spent on the insight. Gridlines, axis labels, legends, and color should each earn their place. If removing an element does not cause the reader to lose meaning, remove it.

These principles apply whether the audience is a branch manager looking at a dashboard or a CFO reviewing a five-year NPV model. The data organization that produces visual communication its audience can interpret quickly and act on confidently earns trust. The one that produces charts requiring explanation loses it.

The Effect of Large Language Models (LLMs) on the Analytics Function

A senior executive recently asked me a question that I was not fully prepared for, though in retrospect I should have been. We were working on an AI project together to create a custom LLM trained on some of her data so she could ask natural language questions. She wanted to know why we could not simply upload the data into Copilot and ask it questions directly. Why did we need to build anything at all? The question itself was not the alarm. What set off the alarm was realizing the wider implications of the path her thinking was taking. She was essentially asking, because from where she sat, the answer was not obvious, whether she needed an analytics group at all. And if it was not obvious to her, it was not obvious to the other executives drawing the same conclusions from the same AI demos happening across every industry. I needed a clear, honest answer, and I needed to be able to give it without sounding defensive.

The appeal of the upload-and-ask approach is real. A business leader who can ask a question of her data in plain English, without waiting for an analyst, without learning SQL, without navigating a dashboard, is more capable than she was two years ago. The floor of analytical accessibility has risen. That is a good thing, and data leaders who dismiss it will lose credibility with the executives they need to influence.

But the upload-and-ask workflow has four failure modes that make it unsuitable as a replacement for governed analytical infrastructure, particularly for any question that matters:

- **Hallucination**: Large language models do not retrieve facts from a database. They generate text based on patterns learned during training, and those patterns sometimes produce outputs that are fluent, confident, and wrong. This is not a bug that will eventually be patched. It is a structural property of how these systems work. A model asked to summarize a dataset may produce figures that do not appear in the underlying data, presented with the same certainty as everything else is accurate. The business leader who does not know to look for this will not catch it. And because the output looks authoritative, she has no reason to question it.

- **The data quality problem**: When a leader uploads an Excel file, the LLM has no way of knowing whether the data is accurate, complete, or consistent with how the same concepts are defined elsewhere in the organization. It does not know that the revenue column excludes returns before a certain date, that the customer count methodology changed in Q3, or that the southeast region numbers have a known quality issue. It will produce a confident, well-formatted answer regardless.
- **The governance problem**: When a business leader uploads company data to a third-party LLM, that data may have left the organization's security perimeter. Access controls, lineage documentation, and security protocols that govern an internal analytics platform do not apply to a consumer chat interface. The convenience comes with risks that most leaders have not fully considered before they have already taken them.
- **The complexity problem**: Most consequential business questions cannot be answered by querying a single file. They require joining data from multiple systems, applying business logic that exists nowhere in a single dataset, and interpreting results in organizational contexts that require domain expertise. An LLM asked those questions without that context will produce an answer. It will not produce the right answer. And

beneath the complexity problem is a judgment problem that is harder to explain but more important. A good analyst answers the question behind the question. They tell you when you are asking the wrong question, when the data cannot support the conclusion you are drawing, and when the answer is technically correct but misleading given what you need to know. That judgment cannot be automated, because it requires understanding what the business is trying to decide.

The Right Way to Use LLM's

The answer to my executive's question was not "you cannot use Copilot." It was "not like that, and here is how we build it so it works."

The data organization's job in this environment is to build the governed, trusted infrastructure that makes first-order analysis safe to do without an analyst in the room. That means connecting LLMs to your organization's data through RAG architectures built on a well-governed semantic layer, with documented definitions, quality guarantees, and access controls. It means building internal AI applications that give business leaders the ability to ask natural language questions of your data and get answers they can trust, because the underlying data has been prepared, validated, and governed by people who understand it.

When that infrastructure exists, something valuable happens. The routine first-order questions like "What were our sales last month?", "Which accounts are at risk?", and "How is this region tracking against plan?" are answered instantly and accurately without requiring analyst time. That frees the analytics function to do what it was always supposed to do: the second- and third-order work that changes how the business operates. Why did sales decline in that region? What should we do about it? What does the data suggest we are missing? Which of our assumptions about customer behavior are wrong?

LLMs used correctly do not replace the analytics function. They remove the lower-value work that was consuming it, and redirect human analytical capacity toward the questions that require human judgment.

That is a better outcome for the business, a better outcome for analysts, and a significantly more defensible position for you to take than simply arguing that the old way was fine.

Augmented and Agentic Analytics

The BI landscape is undergoing a fundamental shift driven by AI. Augmented analytics, a term Gartner coined in 2017,[28] describes

[28] Gartner, "Augmented Analytics," Gartner Glossary, gartner.com.

the use of machine learning and natural language processing to automate and augment insight generation. The most visible manifestation today is natural language querying. Type a question in plain English and receive a data-grounded answer with a supporting visualization, without writing SQL. Every leading BI platform now offers this: Microsoft Copilot for Power BI, Tableau Agent, Google Looker's Gemini-powered conversational analytics, and ThoughtSpot's Spotter. This is table stakes, not a differentiating feature.

The frontier beyond augmented analytics is what practitioners are calling agentic analytics, AI systems that do not just answer questions but proactively analyze data, surface insights without being asked, and in some cases trigger actions or recommendations autonomously. Where traditional BI is pull and augmented analytics is push, agentic analytics is autonomous. Gartner has predicted that AI agents will come to augment or automate roughly half of all business decisions.[29]

For data leaders, the practical implication is clear. The BI function over the next five years will look meaningfully different from the one over the last five years. Teams that invest in governing their semantic layer, building data literacy, and positioning analytics as a decision-support capability rather than a report production capability will be well positioned for this shift. Teams that remain

[29] Gartner, "Gartner Announces the Top Data & Analytics Predictions for 2025 and Beyond," press release, gartner.com, 2025.

organized around dashboard production will find themselves competing with AI tools that build dashboards faster and cheaper.

On tools: the Gartner Magic Quadrant for Analytics and Business Intelligence Platforms, published June 2025, named six Leaders: Microsoft (Power BI/Fabric), Salesforce (Tableau), Google (Looker), Oracle Analytics Cloud, Qlik, and ThoughtSpot. Microsoft was positioned furthest right for the seventh consecutive year.[30] For organizations at earlier stages, Sigma offers a spreadsheet-like interface on top of cloud warehouses that is accessible to non-technical business users. Metabase is a widely adopted open-source option.

Further Reading

Foundational works for going deeper on this topic:

Storytelling with Data, by Cole Nussbaumer Knaflic, referenced earlier in this chapter; the fuller treatment of what makes a chart persuasive rather than just accurate.

Good Charts: The HBR Guide to Making Smarter, More Persuasive Data Visualizations, by Scott Berinato, the natural next stop after this chapter's discussion of what makes a chart persuasive.

---

[30] Gartner, Magic Quadrant for Analytics and Business Intelligence Platforms, June 2025.

Competing on Analytics, by Thomas H. Davenport and Jeanne G. Harris, the book that first made the business case for analytics as a competitive strategy, not just a reporting function.

Legacy Paper and Supply: BI and Analytics

Everything built up to this point has been essentially invisible to the business. The governance policies, the data remediation, the architectural design, the ELT pipelines: none of it has produced anything a branch manager can point to and say, that helped me today. That changes now.

Use Case 1 is ready to be delivered.

The gold tables built in the data engineering chapter contain clean, consistent, and governed sales data, organized exactly as the branch-level analysis requires. The job of the BI and analytics function is to turn it into something the business can use.

The first deliverable is a branch performance dashboard. It shows five things: total sales by salesperson for the current month compared to target, account activity broken down by active, at-risk, and inactive status, product categories ranked by revenue contribution in the branch's region, month-over-month trend lines for each metric, and a simple flag for accounts that have not placed an order in thirty days. Nothing on that dashboard requires a data analyst to interpret. A branch manager can open it in the morning, understand their business in two minutes, and know exactly where to focus their attention that day.

On tool selection, Power BI is the practical default for Legacy. It sits at the accessible end of the cost spectrum, particularly for organizations already paying for Microsoft 365 licenses where it is often included at no additional cost. Combined with Legacy's Microsoft-adjacent infrastructure, a user base of branch managers who are not data professionals, and a small team that needs a tool it can stand up and maintain without deep specialization, Power BI delivers what Use Case 1 requires. The tool selection can be revisited as the analytics program matures and Use Cases 2 and 3 introduce more complex requirements.

This is the moment the data organization becomes real to the people it exists to serve.

When you present the first version of the dashboard to Legacy's branch managers, one of them pushes back. The numbers do not match what she has been tracking in her own spreadsheet. That calls for a calm look, not a crisis response. It is an opportunity. You walk through the definitions together. How active accounts are counted, how sales are attributed to salespeople, how the date logic works. In most cases, the dashboard is right and the spreadsheet has an error. In some cases, the dashboard reveals an edge case in the business logic that nobody had thought through. Either way, the conversation is exactly what good BI work produces: a shared understanding of what the data means, built through honest dialogue rather than unquestioned acceptance.

The most important discipline at this stage is resistance to scope creep. The moment the organization sees what the first dashboard can do, the requests will multiply. Every department will want their own view. Every executive will have a metric they want added. The BI team's job is to protect the quality of what already exists while expanding deliberately and in priority order, not to say yes to everything. Trust in data is built one accurate number at a time. A dashboard that shows ten metrics and gets three of them wrong is worse than a dashboard that shows five metrics and gets all five right every day.

The branch managers who were skeptical at the start are beginning to change. Not all of them, and not completely. But the one who pushed back on the first dashboard has started opening it every morning. She mentioned in a leadership meeting last week that she caught a struggling account before the quarter ended and saved the relationship. That is the story the data organization needs more of. It is also the clearest possible evidence that Use Case 1 is working.

The next chapter covers data science and artificial intelligence, the function that takes the foundation built across this entire module and uses it to predict what will happen next, automate decisions, and build the AI capabilities that are redefining what data organizations can accomplish.

SEVEN

Data Science and Artificial Intelligence

No topic in the business world generates more excitement, confusion, investment, and disappointment simultaneously than data science and artificial intelligence. Every major corporation has announced an AI strategy. Every board is asking about it. Every vendor has rebranded something as AI-powered. And yet adoption and value generation are very different things.

McKinsey's State of AI research found that 78% of organizations were using AI in at least one business function, while its separate Superagency report found that only 1% of leaders described their generative AI rollouts as mature. MIT researchers studying generative AI deployments found that 95% of organizations saw no measurable return on investment within six months of launch.[31] Gartner estimates that roughly half of all generative AI proof-of-concept projects are abandoned before they ever reach production.[32]

We are in the most hyped and most misunderstood technological moments in modern business history. For you, that creates both an enormous opportunity and a significant responsibility.

The opportunity is real. AI is not a fad. The economics of machine learning, the capabilities of modern large language models, and the emergence of AI agents that can take action on behalf of users represent genuine step-changes in what organizations can do with their data. The companies that learn to deploy AI thoughtfully, connecting it to real business problems with the right foundations in place, will create durable competitive advantages.

The responsibility is equally real. Your organization is going to look to you for guidance. Executives will ask how they should be using AI. Business units will pitch projects that range from promising to deeply impractical. Vendors will make claims that range from accurate to absurd. Your job is to cut through the noise, ask the right questions, and help your organization invest in AI that works, while protecting it from the investments that will not.

---

31 **Data Science and Artificial Intelligence:** MIT Project NANDA, The GenAI Divide: State of AI in Business 2025 (MIT, 2025).

32 McKinsey & Company, "The State of AI in 2025," McKinsey Global Survey, and McKinsey, "Superagency in the Workplace" report, 2025.

Getting the Definitions Right

The terms data science, artificial intelligence, machine learning, deep learning, and generative AI are related but distinct.

Data Science is a multidisciplinary field combining statistics, programming, domain expertise, and machine learning to extract knowledge and insights from data. The National Academies of Sciences, Engineering, and Medicine defines it as centering on "multidisciplinary and interdisciplinary approaches to extracting knowledge or insights from large quantities of complex data."[33] Think of data science and AI as two deeply overlapping circles rather than one nested inside the other.

Artificial Intelligence is the broadest technical umbrella, building systems that perform tasks typically requiring human-level reasoning, understanding language, recognizing patterns, and making decisions. Everything that follows is a subset of it.

Machine Learning is a subset of AI. Where traditional software follows explicit rules written by programmers, machine learning systems learn patterns from data and use those patterns to make predictions or decisions without being explicitly programmed for each situation. Amazon's recommendation engine does not have

[33] National Academies of Sciences, Engineering, and Medicine, Envisioning the Data Science Discipline: The Undergraduate Perspective (Washington, DC: National Academies Press, 2018).

a rule that says "if the customer buys diapers, suggest formula." It learned that relationship from millions of customer purchases.

Deep Learning is a subset of machine learning that uses artificial neural networks with many layers to learn complex patterns from large amounts of data. It powers image recognition, speech transcription, and most of the impressive AI capabilities of the past decade.

Generative AI is a class of AI systems, primarily built on deep learning, that produce new content rather than just classify or predict: text, images, music, code, and video. NIST's AI 600-1 framework defines it as "the class of AI models that emulate the structure and characteristics of input data in order to generate derived synthetic content."[34]

Large Language Models are the specific type of generative AI that produces text. Trained on massive amounts of text data, they develop a remarkably general capability. Given a prompt, they predict what text should come next. ChatGPT, Claude, Gemini, and Microsoft Copilot are all LLM-based products.

---

34 National Institute of Standards and Technology, Artificial Intelligence Risk Management Framework: Generative Artificial Intelligence Profile (NIST AI 600-1), July 2024.

Key Concepts Every Data Leader Needs

Hallucination is the tendency of LLMs to produce confident, fluent, and plausible-sounding text that is factually wrong. The model does not retrieve facts from a database; it generates text based on learned patterns, and those patterns sometimes produce errors.

Hallucination is not a bug that will eventually be fixed; it is a property of probabilistic text generation.

Any enterprise deployment of LLMs must account for it through grounding, human review, or evaluation pipelines.

Retrieval-Augmented Generation (RAG) is the dominant pattern for enterprise LLM deployment. Rather than relying on the model's internal knowledge, RAG connects the LLM to an external knowledge base. When a user asks a question, the system retrieves the most relevant documents and includes them in the prompt. The LLM generates a response grounded in your actual documentation and data rather than its general training. The vast majority of enterprise AI applications being built today are RAG systems.

Agentic AI is the frontier beyond generative AI. A traditional AI system responds to prompts. You give it input, it produces output. An AI agent goes further. It perceives its environment, makes a plan, selects and uses tools, takes action, observes the results, and adjusts its plan accordingly, all in pursuit of a goal. Gartner projects that 33% of enterprise software applications will include agentic AI by 2028, up from less than 1% in 2024.[35] Gartner also offers a counterweight, predicting that more than 40% of agentic AI projects will ultimately be canceled due to unclear value, uncontrolled costs, and inadequate governance.[36]

The governance questions around agentic AI are not only technical. What decisions should agents be allowed to make autonomously? The governing principle practitioners have converged on is that autonomy should be proportional to reversibility and risk. An agent that drafts an email for human review is low risk. An agent that sends that email on its own is higher risk. An agent that executes financial transactions or deletes data must meet a much higher standard of reliability and human oversight.

MLOps is the discipline of reliably building, deploying, monitoring, and maintaining machine learning models in production. Organizations without MLOps practices build models that sit in notebooks and never reach production, cannot trace which version of a model is running where, and do not know when a model's performance is degrading. The core practices include model versioning, automated retraining pipelines, drift

---

35 Gartner, "Gartner Predicts Over 40% of Agentic AI Projects Will Be Canceled by End of 2027," press release, June 25, 2025, gartner.com.

36 Gartner, "Gartner Predicts Over 40% of Agentic AI Projects Will Be Canceled by End of 2027," press release, gartner.com, 2025.

monitoring, and a model registry that inventories every model in production with ownership and performance documentation.

Responsible AI and Governance

The question of whether AI will be used responsibly is no longer abstract. It is legal, regulatory, and operational.

The **NIST AI Risk Management Framework (AI RMF 1.0)**, released in January 2023, is the de facto U.S. standard for AI governance, organized around four core functions: Govern, Map, Measure, and Manage.[37]

The **EU AI Act** is the world's first comprehensive binding regulation of AI and applies to any organization operating in or selling to the European market. It classifies AI systems by risk level: prohibited systems include social scoring and most real-time biometric surveillance; high-risk systems subject to mandatory requirements include AI used in hiring, credit scoring, medical diagnostics, and law enforcement. Penalties reach 35 million euros or 7% of global annual revenue. Prohibited systems were banned as of February 2025, general-purpose AI obligations took effect in

---

[37] National Institute of Standards and Technology, Artificial Intelligence Risk Management Framework (AI RMF 1.0), January 2023.

August 2025, and full high-risk system requirements apply from August 2026.[38]

AI bias occurs when a model produces systematically different outcomes for different groups in ways that are unfair or discriminatory, almost always because the training data reflected historical human biases or because the model was not tested for differential performance across groups. Unmitigated bias is not inevitable, but it requires deliberate measurement, diverse training data, fairness-aware modeling techniques, and ongoing monitoring in production. Organizations that do not explicitly test for bias will not discover it until it causes harm.

Why AI Projects Fail

The failure statistics contain the most important strategic information available to you right now. RAND's 2024 analysis found that roughly 80% of AI projects fail to deliver their intended business value, approximately twice the failure rate of traditional IT projects.[39] S&P Global found that 42% of companies

---

38 European Union, Regulation (EU) 2024/1689 (Artificial Intelligence Act), Official Journal of the European Union, July 12, 2024.

39 RAND Corporation, "The Root Causes of Failure for Artificial Intelligence Projects" (2024), report no. RRA2680-1.

abandoned most of their AI initiatives in 2025, up from 17% the year before.[40]

What is causing these failures? The research is consistent, and the answer may surprise those who assume AI projects fail due to technical problems. They mostly do not. The most commonly identified causes are misaligned incentives and the absence of end-user involvement in project design; poorly defined business problems; inadequate data foundations; technology-first thinking that skips organizational change planning; and insufficient governance. Every item on that list is an organizational and leadership failure, not a technical one. The models work. What fails is the connection between the technology and the people, processes, and business problems it was supposed to serve.

McKinsey's 2025 research identified a striking pattern. The highest-ROI organizations are twice as likely to have redesigned end-to-end workflows before selecting a modeling technique.[41]

> *They do not start with "what AI can we use" and then look for problems. They start with "what work are we trying to do differently" and then assess whether AI is the right tool.*

[40] S&P Global Market Intelligence, Voice of the Enterprise: AI & Machine Learning, 2025.

[41] McKinsey & Company, "The State of AI: How Organizations Are Rewiring to Capture Value," McKinsey Global Survey, 2025.

Build, Buy, or Partner

A consequential strategic decision you will make about AI is whether to build custom systems, purchase pre-built capabilities, or partner with platform providers. The practical answer for most organizations is all three, for different parts of the AI portfolio.

Buy or use APIs for capabilities that are commoditized and where your data does not need to be in the model. Frontier LLMs available via API represent billions of dollars of research investment you do not need to replicate. General-purpose tools for document summarization, email drafting, code assistance, and language translation are better bought than built for the vast majority of organizations.

Build or adapt where the capability encodes your proprietary advantage. The way you retrieve and synthesize your internal knowledge, the specific signals that predict churn in your customer base, the demand patterns unique to your product mix and geography. These are likely worth building because they represent differentiation that a general-purpose API cannot provide.

Partner with AI platforms for managed infrastructure. Vertex AI, Azure AI Foundry, and Amazon Bedrock offer managed platforms for building, deploying, and monitoring AI applications, combining compute infrastructure, foundation model access, and operational tooling that would take years to build independently.

The decision comes down to four questions: Does this capability encode a proprietary advantage? How sensitive is the data involved? What is the total cost of ownership over three years? And what is the realistic talent requirement to build versus buy?

Further Reading

Foundational works for going deeper on this topic:

Minding the Machines: Building and Leading Data Science and Analytics Teams, by Jeremy Adamson, entirely devoted to leading the team doing this work.

Data Science for Business, by Foster Provost and Tom Fawcett, still the clearest explanation of what data science is for a business reader, machine learning included.

Prediction Machines: The Simple Economics of Artificial Intelligence, by Ajay Agrawal, Joshua Gans, and Avi Goldfarb, reframes AI as a drop in the cost of prediction, a useful mental model for deciding where it applies.

Legacy Paper and Supply: Data Science and AI

The AI conversation at Legacy has already started without you. The Chief Executive Officer (CEO) attended an industry conference and came back convinced the company needs to "do something with AI." The head of sales wants to know if a tool exists that can tell him which accounts are at risk before he loses them. The warehouse manager saw a vendor demo of an AI-powered forecasting system and sent you a link with three exclamation points. Everyone is excited. Nobody has asked whether Legacy has the data foundations, the talent, the governance structures, or the problem definition clarity required to make any of this work.

That is precisely where your job begins.

The good news is that the work done across the previous five chapters has built exactly the foundation that data science and AI require. The governance chapter established ownership and definitions. The data management chapter cleaned and standardized the customer and transaction records. The architecture chapter designed the dimensional model. The engineering chapter built the pipelines and gold tables. The BI chapter put the first trusted dashboard in front of the business. Legacy is not starting from scratch. It is ready for the next layer.

Building the Demand Forecasting Model

Use Case 2 is the natural first data science project. The work begins not with modeling but with data preparation, because the quality of the training data determines the ceiling of what the model can achieve.

The training dataset needs to be constructed carefully. The core is daily order volume by product and branch, pulled from the gold layer. But raw transaction history is not enough. The model needs features, variables that help it understand the patterns driving demand. For Legacy, the most important are seasonality indicators capturing time of year, day of week, and proximity to holidays; branch-level characteristics capturing customer mix and regional conditions; product-level characteristics capturing category and historical volatility; and lag features capturing what demand looked like in the prior week, month, and quarter. Building those features requires close collaboration between the data scientist and the procurement team, because the people who have managed inventory manually for years carry institutional knowledge of demand patterns that no dataset captures on its own.

For a distribution company at Legacy's scale, a gradient boosting model or a time series approach like Prophet is a reasonable starting point. Neither requires deep machine learning expertise, and both are interpretable enough that the procurement team can understand why the model is making a particular prediction, which matters enormously for adoption. A model whose outputs nobody trusts will not be used regardless of its accuracy.

Validation means testing predictions against a holdout period of historical data, ideally the most recent three to six months, and comparing accuracy against the current manual forecasting process. If the model outperforms the status quo on a metric the procurement team recognizes, such as forecast error rate or stockout frequency, you have a concrete case for production deployment.

Deployment means delivering the model's output to the people who need to act on it. The most practical approach is a weekly forecast report in Power BI alongside the branch performance dashboard, predicted demand by product and branch for the next four to eight weeks, flagged against current inventory levels, with highlighted exceptions where stockout risk is high. No new tool, no new workflow, just better information in a place they already look.

Monitor the model after deployment. Demand patterns change, a new competitor enters a market, a product gets discontinued, a major customer changes their ordering behavior. A model trained on historical data will gradually drift as the world diverges from what it was trained on. Establish accuracy metrics from day one, review them monthly, and build a retraining cadence into the team's operating rhythm. A model that was accurate a year ago and has never been revisited can become a liability, not an asset.

Building the Customer and Account Intelligence Application

Use Case 3 is the AI application that gives sales reps and branch managers the ability to ask natural-language questions about their customers and receive reliable, immediate answers. Which of my accounts have not ordered in sixty days? Which customers in the northeast are spending less than they were this time last year?

What products did our top ten accounts buy last quarter that they have not reordered yet?

These questions are answerable today, but only if you know how to query a database or navigate the dashboard in exactly the right way. Most branch managers do not. The result is that they either do not ask the question, or they add it to an analyst's queue and hear back three days later. By then the moment has passed.

The architecture is RAG. A large language model is connected to Legacy's customer and account data through a structured interface. When a sales rep asks a question in plain English, the system retrieves the relevant data and uses the LLM to formulate a clear, accurate answer. The LLM is not guessing or drawing on general knowledge. It is reading Legacy's actual data and summarizing what it finds.

Three things need to be true before this application can go live. First, the underlying data needs to meet a higher-quality bar than in other use cases. A dashboard that shows a slightly wrong number gives the user context to question it. A confident natural language answer that is wrong gives them nothing but misinformation. Second, the semantic layer needs to be well documented. The LLM needs to understand what Legacy's data means, the business concepts behind the columns, how each field is calculated, and what each valid value represents. The data glossary from the governance chapter is the starting point. Third, guardrails need to be in place before the application reaches sales reps. It should only answer questions about data it has access to, every answer should reference the underlying data it drew from, and it should say "I don't know" when the required data is not available rather than generating a plausible-sounding but fabricated response.

The rollout should start small. Pilot with two or three branch managers who are technically comfortable and willing to give honest feedback. Run it in parallel with the existing process for thirty days. Fix what breaks. Expand when the accuracy and trust bar has been met. A broad rollout of an application that sales reps do not trust is harder to recover from than a slow rollout of one they do.

Sequencing and What Comes Next

The demand forecasting model should go into production first. It has a clear, measurable outcome; it operates in the background rather than interacting directly with end users, and it trains the organization to trust model-driven recommendations before it encounters the more novel experience of conversational AI. Use Case 3 follows once the data quality bar is high enough and once the organization has developed enough AI literacy to use it well and recognize when it is wrong.

The most important thing to resist at Legacy is the pressure to skip steps. The CEO's enthusiasm is an asset, but it needs to be managed. Your job is to channel that energy toward the right investments in the right order, protect the organization from expensive experiments it is not yet ready for, and build AI capability that lasts.

This chapter closes Part 1. You now have a working understanding of each of the core functions of a data organization and how they fit together. Part 2 turns from understanding the functions to building the organization, starting with data strategy, the plan that determines what you build, in what order, and why.

PART II

Building Data Organizations

Part 1 was about understanding. You now know what a data organization is, what each of its functions does, how the pieces connect, and why each one matters. You understand what good data governance looks like, what a well-designed data architecture enables, and what a mature data engineering practice makes possible. That foundation is necessary, and now it gets put to use.

Part 2 is about doing.

The three chapters that follow are not descriptive. They are operational. They will walk you through the three most important things you build. A strategy that tells the organization where it is going and how it will get there, a set of processes that make winning repeatable, and a team with the skills to execute. Jeremy Adamson, in *Minding the Machines: Building and Leading Data Science and Analytics Teams*, frames the work of building a successful analytics organization around three pillars: strategy, process, and people. That framing has influenced my own philosophy, and it is how this module is organized. If you want to go deeper on his approach to the three pillars and building data science and analytics teams after reading this book, his book is worth your time. These are the chapters where the knowledge from Part 1 gets put to work.

We start with strategy, because everything else depends on it. You cannot hire the right people without knowing what you need them to do. You cannot design the right processes without knowing what outcomes they are supposed to produce. You cannot make good architecture decisions without knowing what business problems the architecture is supposed to solve. Strategy is the organizing logic that gives everything else its direction. You have spent Part 1 learning what a data organization looks like from the inside. Now it is time to build the plan.

EIGHT

Building a Data Strategy

Most data leaders arrive in their role with strong opinions about technology. What they often underestimate is how much of the job is strategy, not technology. And strategy, for many technically trained people, is an uncomfortable place to operate.

Strategy requires making choices before you have complete information. It requires committing to a direction when reasonable people disagree. It requires translating abstract business goals into specific, funded, staffed initiatives. And it requires persuading people who did not ask for your help that your plan is worth their time, attention, and budget.

A data strategy is not a technology roadmap. It is the organizing logic for how your organization will create value from its data and AI assets. It answers three questions: Where are you now, where do you want to go, and how will you get there? Organizations that do this well transform their data function from a cost center into a value generator, moving from reactive to proactive. Organizations that skip it build impressive-looking technical infrastructure that never quite connects to the problems the business is trying to solve. They hire talented people who spend their time on the wrong things. They make expensive investments that produce spreadsheets rather than decisions.

What a Data Strategy Is

Synthesizing what Gartner, MIT, IBM, and McKinsey have converged on: a data strategy is a dynamic, business-aligned plan that defines how an organization will create value from its data and AI assets, articulating vision, priorities, capabilities, governance, and roadmap, and is implemented through a corresponding operating model.

Three phrases matter. "Dynamic" means a data strategy is not a document you write once and file. The business changes, the technology changes, new AI capabilities emerge. A data strategy that was excellent in 2023 will be insufficient in 2026. It must be treated as a living framework, revisited at least annually. The organizations that fail most reliably are those whose strategy is laminated rather than maintained.

"Business-aligned" means the data strategy derives its purpose entirely from the business strategy. Every priority should trace back to a business outcome someone in the C-suite cares about. If you cannot draw that line, question whether the initiative belongs in the strategy at all.

"Operating model" means a strategy without one is a vision without execution. The operating model defines how the work gets done, who owns what decisions about data, how the data team is organized relative to the business, and how priorities are set and funded. Many beautifully written data strategies fail because they describe a future state without specifying the organizational mechanics required to reach it.

The Offense and Defense Balance

The data management chapter introduced the offense and defense framework. In strategy work, it becomes a decision-making tool for allocating investment.

The pressure you will feel from executives and business partners will pull you almost entirely toward offense. Build the dashboard, ship the model, show the ROI. That pressure is real, but giving in to it completely is a trap. Data organizations that skip the defensive foundation in the rush to deliver visible results find those results becoming unreliable, ungoverned, and ultimately distrusted. The best data strategies build enough defense to operate responsibly while generating enough offensive value to sustain the funding and executive support required to continue.

DalleMule and Davenport, whose 2017 Harvard Business Review piece introduced the framework, put it well: the right balance depends on the organization. A heavily regulated financial institution may need to run 70% defensive before it can invest in offense. A consumer technology company with a lighter regulatory burden may run at 70% offensive.[42] Most organizations fall somewhere in between, and the balance shifts as they mature.

The Three Questions

All data strategy work comes back to three questions: Where are we now, where do we want to go, and how do we get there? The rest of this chapter walks through each in depth, then through the work of translating the answers into a formal strategy document and a presentation to senior leadership.

Question 1: Where Are We Now?

The current state assessment serves as the foundation for the strategy. You cannot define a meaningful future state without an honest picture of the present, and you cannot build organizational credibility without demonstrating that you understood the business before prescribing solutions.

---

[42] **Building a Data Strategy:** Lak DalleMule and Thomas H. Davenport, "What's Your Data Strategy?" Harvard Business Review, May–June 2017.

This is also where many data leaders rush. Resist it. Organizations that skip the assessment and jump to recommendations spend money on solutions to problems they do not actually have while ignoring the problems they do.

I once worked with a Chief Data Officer who understood this better than anyone I have encountered since. When he joined the organization, he spent the first three months doing almost nothing but asking questions. At every meeting, he was in the room, listening. When he spoke, it was never to judge or prescribe. He said something once that has stayed with me: "Everything that is happening made sense to someone when it started." His job, as he saw it, was to find that logic before he touched anything. He understood that walking into a complex system and making changes without understanding it first is a reliable way to break things that were quietly working. By the time he was ready to act, he knew exactly what needed to change and why. A good current state assessment is the first step in the real work itself, not a box to check before it begins.

The assessment covers five domains:

1. **Data sources and inventory:** What data does the organization have, where does it live, who owns it, and what business processes does it support? This exercise almost always produces surprises. Systems nobody mentioned in initial interviews turn out to be critical, and data leaders assumed was being captured turns out not to exist in any systematic form.

2. **Data quality:** How accurate, complete, consistent, and timely is the data central to the priority use cases? Pay particular attention to workarounds; when people have adapted to a quality problem, it does not mean the problem is small. It means it has become invisible.

3. **Governance and management maturity:** Does a data governance program exist in practice, not just on paper? Are there data owners with real accountability? Is there a business glossary that is actually used? For organizations that want a scored assessment, the CMMI Data Management Maturity model, the EDM Council's DCAM, and the Gartner Data and Analytics Maturity Model all provide consistent frameworks that give the findings an external reference point.[43]

4. **Infrastructure and architecture:** What technology is currently in use, and does it support the business's data needs? The question is not which platform the organization uses but whether the infrastructure is reliable, governable, scalable, and aligned to what the business needs to do.

5. **Data culture and skills:** How data-literate is the broader workforce? Do business leaders routinely consult data

---

[43] CMMI Institute, Data Management Maturity Model; EDM Council, Data Management Capability Assessment Model (DCAM); Gartner, Data and Analytics Maturity Model.

before making decisions, or do they reach for gut instinct and use data to confirm decisions already made? The Wavestone Data and AI Leadership Executive Survey, which has asked Fortune 1000 data leaders about the barriers to becoming data-driven for more than a decade, points the same direction every year. The primary obstacle is culture, people, and process, not technology. In the 2025 survey, 92% of respondents identified people and organizational change as the main barrier, while only 8% identified technology.[44] Organizations that invest heavily in platforms while neglecting literacy, training, and cultural change consistently underperform their peers.

Question 2: Where Do We Want to Go?

The single most important discipline in future-state visioning is starting with what the business needs to achieve, not with what the data team wants to build. Data leaders excited about technology often start from a capability wish list. A real-time data platform, a unified customer data model, an AI experimentation framework. These may all be excellent investments. But if the starting point is the capability rather than the business outcome, the strategy will always struggle to justify itself in executive terms.

---

[44] Wavestone, 2025 AI & Data Leadership Executive Benchmark Survey (Wavestone, 2025), formerly published by NewVantage Partners.

The right starting point is conversations with business leaders: What are the most important problems you are trying to solve, what decisions do you make today on incomplete information, where are competitors using data in ways that give them an advantage? From those conversations, distill a prioritized set of business use cases: specific, measurable applications of data and analytics that directly support a business objective. "Improve sales analytics" is not a use case. "Identify customers with declining engagement 60 days before churn, enabling the sales team to intervene and retain accounts worth an average of $47,000 annually" is a use case. The specificity determines whether it gets funded, whether success can be measured, and whether the people who need to act will do so.

Question 3: How Do We Get There?

Gap analysis is the structured process of comparing where the organization is now with where it needs to be, identifying specific capability deficits between the two, and prioritizing them by business impact and feasibility. Rigorous gap analysis involves scoring each capability dimension on a consistent scale, prioritizing by which business outcomes each gap blocks, mapping dependencies (you cannot build a reliable forecasting model until you have clean training data; you cannot have clean data without governance), and sizing the cost and expected value of each gap-closure initiative.

Five pitfalls undermine gap analyses in practice: technology-first thinking that names "we need a new platform" as a gap rather than the business capability the platform enables; over-breadth that tries to assess every dataset rather than focusing on priority domains; treating culture and skills as residual while addressing only technical gaps; failing to distinguish must-haves from should-haves; and ignoring AI readiness entirely.

Vision, Mission, and Values

A data strategy describes where the organization is going and how it will get there. A vision, mission, and set of values describe why it matters and how the organization will operate along the way. These should be developed with genuine input from the people who will live inside them. A vision written alone in a weekend and presented on Monday is a document. A vision that emerged from real conversations is an organizational commitment.

Vision describes the future the data organization is working toward, anchored in what the data organization aspires to enable for the business. A good vision is specific enough to be evaluated. "To be a world-class data organization that delivers innovative data-driven insights" contains no information. "A Legacy Paper and Supply where every branch manager starts their day with a clear picture of their business, where procurement never runs short of a product because the data said it was coming, and where any sales rep can get an answer about any customer in thirty seconds" describes a future state the organization can recognize when it arrives.

A mission describes the day-to-day purpose of a data organization. Not "to leverage data and analytics to drive transformational business value through cutting-edge technology," which could describe any function anywhere, but "to build and maintain the data capabilities that give Legacy's business leaders the information they need to make confident decisions, and to do it in a way that is trustworthy, accessible, and continuously improving."

Values describe how the organization will operate when the situation is ambiguous. The test of a useful value is whether it would cause someone to make a different decision than they otherwise would have made. "Integrity: we act with honesty and transparency" tells no one anything specific. "We say what the data actually shows, even when it is not what the business wants to hear" tells a data analyst exactly what to do when a senior leader pushes back on findings that contradict their preferred narrative. Some values worth building into a data organization include intellectual honesty about what the data can and cannot support, healthy skepticism toward results that look too clean or confirm exactly what was expected, transparency about uncertainty and the limitations of analysis, and a bias toward delivering something useful rather than waiting for perfect.

The Formal Strategy Document

The work of assessment, visioning, gap analysis, and roadmap ultimately gets documented in a formal strategy document. A complete document has at least these 12 components.

The **executive summary** gives everyone who will not read the full document what they need: the strategic vision in plain language, the two or three most important business outcomes, the top priority initiatives, the investment ask, and the key success metrics. Two to three pages, no technical specifications.

The **business context** section demonstrates that you understand the business before prescribing solutions. It describes the organization's competitive environment, strategic priorities, and the specific business goals the data strategy is designed to support. A strategy document that opens with technical capabilities before establishing business context signals the data team is building what interests them rather than what the business needs.

The **current state assessment** section documents the findings from the assessment described above. It should be honest. A current-state assessment that characterizes everything as "reasonably mature" when the actual state is primitive will yield a strategy too timid to drive real change.

The **future-state vision** describes what the organization's data capabilities, culture, and operating model will look like once the strategy has been successfully executed. A useful future state makes specific claims: not "we will be a data-driven organization" but "in 24 months, every significant commercial decision at Legacy can be informed by data from a trusted, governed platform."

The **data strategy objectives** translate the future state into SMART goals. Good objectives sound like: "Reduce the time to produce monthly financial reports from five days to one day by Q4." Bad objectives sound like: "Improve data quality across the organization." Directions are not destinations.

The **roadmap** sequences the investments required to close the gap between current and future state. It organizes initiatives into phases, with defined timelines. Each initiative traces back to a business use case it enables, includes resource requirements in people and budget, acknowledges dependencies, and has a cadence for review and revision. A strategy document without a roadmap is a vision without a path.

The **data use-case portfolio** is often absent from strategy templates but is what executives most want to see. It documents the specific, prioritized business use cases the strategy is designed to enable, each with the business problem it addresses, the data it requires, the expected business value, and the dependency chain that determines when it can be executed.

The **data governance framework** describes who is accountable for which data domains, how decisions are made and issues escalated, and what policies govern data access, quality, and compliance. A strategy that describes ambitious analytics and AI capabilities without a governance framework is a plan to build a skyscraper on sand.

The **data architecture** section describes the target state of the data infrastructure at a level of abstraction appropriate for a business audience, what the technology stack will look like and why each choice was made, without requiring the reader to understand implementation details.

The **data analytics and AI** section describes the analytics capabilities the organization will build and the AI use-case portfolio. IBM's 2025 Chief Data Officer study, based on 1,700 data leaders worldwide, found that 81% now integrate their data strategy with their technology and infrastructure roadmap, up from 52% in 2023,[45] evidence that AI and data strategy are converging rather than living in separate plans. A data strategy that treats AI as a future aspiration rather than a current planning requirement is already behind the field.

The **data security and privacy** section demonstrates that the organization takes its data protection obligations seriously, including the regulatory requirements it faces, the data classification scheme, access control policies, encryption standards, and the incident response plan.

---

[45] IBM Institute for Business Value, in cooperation with Oxford Economics, 2025 Chief Data Officer Study, based on a survey of 1,700 data and analytics leaders across 27 geographies, November 2025.

The **talent and skills plan** articulates the competency profile the organization needs, where those competencies currently exist, and how the gaps will be closed through hiring, training, and organizational development. It should also address data literacy for the broader workforce, the investment required to build the capability across the business to read, interpret, and act on data outputs without requiring an analyst to translate at every step. The data team can build the best analytics program in the industry and still fail if the people it is supposed to serve do not have the literacy to use it. The hiring and leading data talent chapter covers this in depth; the strategy document should include enough detail to make clear that the human investment has been thought through.

The **change management plan** is the most frequently omitted component and the most frequently cited cause of failure when it is missing. A data strategy is a behavioral transformation that involves technology. It asks people across the organization to make decisions differently, follow new processes, and trust information sources they may not have relied on before. None of that happens automatically. The plan describes how the organization will communicate the strategy, equip people to work in the new environment, and manage resistance. Organizations that invest in change management alongside technical implementation are substantially more likely to realize the value their data strategies project.

Always Create a One-Pager

No matter how thorough the full strategy document, you need to be able to summarize it on a single page. Many of the people whose support the strategy needs will not read a thirty-page document.

An effective one-pager leads with the strategic vision in one or two sentences in business language, follows with two or three priority business outcomes, presents the top five to seven use cases each tied to a time horizon, shows a simple representation of the current-versus-target maturity gap, states the investment ask, and closes with three to five success metrics. Curation, not compression, is the goal.

Presenting to Senior Leadership

Building the strategy is the first challenge. Getting it approved and funded is often the harder one. Here are some pointers:

- **Lead with the answer, not the analysis**: The most common mistake data leaders make in executive presentations is walking through background and findings before the recommendation. Executives want to know what you are recommending, why, and what they need to do. State the recommendation first.
- **Speak the audience's language**: A CFO cares about ROI and risk. A Chief Marketing Officer (CMO) cares about

customer acquisition and retention. A Chief Operating Officer (COO) cares about efficiency and reliability. Technical vocabulary belongs only if the audience is known to be technically fluent.

- **Quantify the value**: "Improving demand forecasting will reduce inventory carrying costs by an estimated $1.2M annually, based on our current carrying rate and improvement observed at comparable distributors" is specific and defensible. Abstract benefit claims are forgettable. But be careful, specificity is a commitment as much as it is a strength. An executive who hears $1.2M will likely remember it long after the assumptions behind it are forgotten. Make sure the number can survive scrutiny if someone challenges the methodology, and make sure the initiative can actually deliver it, because missing a number you put in front of leadership costs you far more credibility than a vaguer claim ever would have.

- **Use the SCQA framework** (Situation, Complication, Question, Answer): The Situation establishes shared context. The Complication introduces the tension that makes action necessary. The Question names what the audience is about to consider. The Answer is the recommendation. Every supporting element serves that answer.

- **Apply the so-what test:** For every finding, keep asking "so what?" until the answer is something an executive cares about, not just something that changed. More on this discipline, and why most reporting stops short of it, in the Stakeholder Management chapter.

- **Acknowledge trade-offs**: Executives are skeptical of strategies that present only upside. A presentation that acknowledges what the strategy will not do, what it will cost, and what risks it carries is more credible than one that promises everything.

Why Data Strategies Fail

A Wavestone survey found that only 24% of organizations describe themselves as data driven.[46] CDO tenure averages roughly two to three years, shorter than nearly every other C-suite role. These failures are not primarily technical. They are organizational.

The most common causes include a lack of business alignment and a tendency to build what the data team finds interesting rather than what solves business problems. Another cause is treating the strategy as a one-time deliverable rather than a living framework. Technology-first thinking also causes strategies to be defined around platform migrations rather than business outcomes. Organizations also fail when they underinvest in culture, people,

---

46 Wavestone, AI & Data Leadership Executive Benchmark Survey.

and process. The absence of measurable business outcomes means the strategy cannot survive budget pressure. Without an executive sponsor (CEO, COO, or CFO) who actively advocates for the strategy in budget discussions and uses its outputs in their own decision-making, a data strategy depends entirely on your personal credibility to survive. If there is a misalignment with IT the data architecture depends on IT infrastructure, the data governance program depends on IT systems, and a data strategy developed in isolation from the IT strategy produces conflicts that consume organizational energy. And, in 2025 and 2026, ignoring AI readiness. IBM's 2025 CDO study found that only 26% of data leaders are confident their data can support AI-enabled revenue streams.[47] The other 74% have a gap that will constrain their AI ambitions regardless of how sophisticated their analytics capabilities become.

Further Reading

Foundational works for going deeper on this topic:

The Chief Data Officer's Playbook, by Caroline Carruthers and Peter Jackson, the source of the Immediate Data Strategy and Target Data Strategy framework used throughout this book.

---

[47] IBM Institute for Business Value, 2025 Chief Data Officer Study (November 2025).

Data Strategy and the Enterprise Data Executive, by Peter Aiken and Todd Harbour, a practical treatment of data as a strategic asset, written specifically for the executive who has to make the case for it.

Humanizing Data Strategy, by Tiankai Feng, a reminder that even the most technical strategy document is ultimately a human artifact, aimed at human stakeholders.

Legacy Paper and Supply: Data Strategy

Before the governance policies were written, before the first pipeline was built, before the branch dashboard went live, there were conversations.

In your first weeks at Legacy, you met with every business leader, the VP of Sales, the heads of the five regional branches, the CFO, the COO, and the CEO. You were not presenting anything. You were listening. What decisions do you make today on incomplete information? Where are you operating blind? What would you do differently if you trusted your numbers more?

Those conversations produced Legacy's Immediate Data Strategy, three use cases addressing the most urgent business pain, deliverable with available resources, designed to demonstrate enough value quickly enough to earn the organizational trust and budget needed to do something more ambitious. The IDS was never meant to be the destination. It was designed to buy time, time to build the foundation, establish credibility, and develop a Target Data Strategy (TDS) that defines where Legacy is going over the next three to five years.

That work happens in parallel with IDS execution. While the data engineer builds pipelines and the analyst develops dashboards, you continue the conversation with the business. By month six, you have documented twenty-three use cases across the organization, from relatively quick analytical wins to multi-year AI initiatives. Not all will make it into the TDS; some will be deprioritized because the data does not yet exist, some will be consolidated, and some will be deferred because the capability they require depends on infrastructure still under construction. But twenty-three documented use cases, each tied to a specific business leader and business problem, means the TDS is grounded in real organizational demand.

Conducting the Current State Assessment

The assessment covers the five domains described earlier and takes approximately four weeks. The data source inventory produces a four-system picture: Salesforce, the order management platform, QuickBooks, and Workday. The data quality findings are less encouraging. Salesforce account status is populated in only 67% of records, and the values that are populated are inconsistent because nobody ever agreed on what they should be. QuickBooks has three different naming conventions for the same product category applied across different time periods. The order management platform is the cleanest system in the estate, with greater than 95% completeness across all critical fields.

The governance maturity score comes back at 1.2 out of 5, essentially no program in place. No data owners, no business glossary, no documented policies, no lineage. Infrastructure maturity is not much better at 1.5; the systems exist but are not integrated. Skills and culture land at 2.0. There is one capable analyst and reasonable executive openness to data, but no data literacy program and significant variation in how willing different leaders are to change their decision-making behavior.

Gap Analysis and Business Value

The gap analysis maps the distance between where Legacy is and where it needs to be for each use case. For sales performance visibility, the gap is primarily infrastructure and governance. A data warehouse, ELT connectors, a dimensional model, a BI tool, and agreed-upon metric definitions. For demand forecasting, the gap is data quality and data science capability. Three years of clean transaction history, feature engineering, a model, and a deployment process. For customer and account intelligence, the gap is all of the above plus a semantic layer and an AI application layer, making it a 12-18 month commitment rather than a day-one priority.

The dependency mapping is the most important output of the gap analysis. Governance must come before quality remediation, quality remediation before reliable analytics, reliable analytics before AI. The sequence is not arbitrary. Each layer is a prerequisite for the next. If you try to skip governance and go straight to AI, you'll build an impressive-looking application on an unstable foundation and spend the next 18 months explaining why it keeps producing wrong answers.

Every use case in the strategy document should have a rough dollar value assigned to it. For sales performance visibility, you sit with the VP of Sales. How many accounts does Legacy lose each year that could have been saved with earlier intervention? He estimates fifteen to twenty. Average annual value of a lost account? The CFO's data shows $47,000. Conservatively, fifteen accounts retained at $47,000 each is $705,000 in protected revenue annually, presented as a range of $500,000 to $900,000 depending on retention rate assumptions. That is a target and a basis for conversation, not a guarantee.

For demand forecasting, conversations with the COO and head of procurement surface a combined annual drag of $800,000 to $1.2 million from stockouts and excess inventory. A forecasting model that reduces that drag by 30% produces $240,000 to $360,000 in annual savings, again presented as a range with the assumptions visible.

For customer and account intelligence, the value at this stage is best presented qualitatively. 40 sales reps saving two hours per week on account research is 4,160 hours annually redirected to selling activity. You note that this use case also has the highest dependency on the first two, indicating that its value depends on getting the foundation right.

The Presentation

The strategy is shared with stakeholders days before the formal presentation, giving them time to formulate their initial questions before they are in the room, so the presentation can be a conversation rather than a briefing. The presentation itself runs for 18 minutes and opens with the SCQA framing: "Legacy has been growing successfully for 40 years on the strength of relationships and reputation." The data environment has not kept pace, and competitors are using capabilities Legacy does not have. Branch managers are losing accounts they could have retained, procurement is leaving money on the table, and sales reps are spending time on account research instead of selling. How should Legacy invest in data to protect and grow its market position? Here is the recommendation.

The CEO's first question is about ROI. You walk through the dollar ranges and the assumptions behind them. The CFO's first question is about timeline. You show the dependency map and explain why the sequence cannot be compressed without increasing risk. The VP of Sales wants to know how the customer intelligence application will work in practice. You explain the pilot approach: two branches, thirty days, honest evaluation before any broader rollout.

The strategy is approved, with a modest adjustment to the year-one timeline to accommodate a parallel CRM cleanup initiative the COO has already committed to. The data strategy is funded. The easiest part is done.

The next chapter covers processes, the operating rhythms, governance structures, and execution disciplines that determine whether a well-built strategy gets delivered.

NINE

Developing Processes

James Clear opens his book *Atomic Habits* with an observation that applies just as well to organizations as it does to individuals: every Olympic athlete wants the gold medal. Every single one of them, without exception. The goal isn't what separated the athlete who reached the podium from the rest of the field, since everyone standing at the starting line wanted precisely the same thing. What separated them was what they did every single day in the years before that race. The training, the recovery, the small repeatable systems that held up long after the initial motivation to compete had faded into routine. Organizations operate the same way.

You now have a strategy. You have documented where your organization is today, articulated where you want it to go, and built a roadmap with specific initiatives, timelines, and resource requirements. Leadership has signed off. But every competitor in your market wants the same thing you do: faster insight, better decisions, a real advantage from its data, and none of that is what will separate you from them either. What determines whether you get there is not the strategy document leadership just signed. It is what your organization does the same way, every day, long after the energy of that signature has worn off. That is what process is, and it is the difference between a strategy that becomes real and one that quietly dies at the starting line.

A strategy without process is a wish without a mechanism. Strategy tells you what you are trying to accomplish. Process is how you make accomplishing it repeatable, reliable, and survivable even when the people who originally built it leave.

If your organization can only produce good results when specific individuals are available, in the right mood, and happen to remember how something was done six months ago, you do not have an organization. You have a dependency on people rather than a capability in the institution. Processes convert individual knowledge and informal habits into organizational capability, on purpose, rather than by accident. That is the difference between a data team that scales and one that perpetually re-invents itself.

What Makes a Bad Process

Bad processes are not rare. They accumulate through years of improvisation, organizational change, and the human tendency to solve today's problem without thinking about tomorrow's.

A bad process is inefficient, wasting time, resources, or effort on steps that exist for historical reasons that no longer apply. It is ineffective; it fails to produce the desired outcome. It is inconsistent because two people following the same nominal process produce different results when the process was never documented carefully enough. It is overly complex, with more steps and approvals than the outcome warrants, which causes people to work around it and produces the very inconsistency the complexity was meant to prevent. And it resists change, designed for a world that no longer exists, with no one holding the authority or motivation to update it.

There is also such a thing as too much process. A task that takes thirty minutes to complete and an hour to document and route through approval is not rigor. It is a tax, and the team pays it on every single occurrence, forever. Not everything deserves a process. Some things are fine left to individual judgment, done a little differently by different people, with no template and no sign-off. Every hour your team spends on process administration is an hour it is not spending on the work that produces value, and that tradeoff is worth making deliberately, not by default.

The Leader's Role in Process

Your job in process is not always design. Someone else can map the swimlane diagram, write the RACI matrix, document the steps. What a leader alone controls is whether any of it actually becomes how the team behaves, and that happens through a narrower set of levers than most leaders realize: what you pay attention to in a status update, how you react the day something actually breaks, whether you protect the time a process needs when a deadline gets tight, and whether you follow the process yourself when it would be easier not to. A team that watches its leader ask about process compliance only when convenient, or quietly wave it aside under pressure, learns the real rule within a week, whatever the documentation says.

Processes fail most often not because they were poorly designed but because leaders announced them without reinforcing them. The announcement gets compliance for a few weeks. Then the first crisis arrives, someone skips a step because there is no time, the leader says nothing, and within a month the process exists only on paper. The most important single thing a leader can do for process execution is to visibly use the processes themselves.

Managing Demand and Ad-Hoc Work

There is one process failure that will sink a data function faster than any other, and it is not a broken pipeline or a missed deadline. It is the failure to manage demand.

The math is unforgiving. Demand for data work is effectively infinite after your team proves its capabilities and value. Every executive has a question, every team wants a dashboard, every new hire arrives with a list of things that should be automated. Capacity is finite and grows slowly. The gap between the two is permanent, and how you manage that gap determines whether your team is seen as a strategic partner or a perpetually late order-taker. A team with no mechanism for choosing what to work on will be chosen for by whoever is loudest, most senior, or most recently in the room. That is not a strategy. It is surrender dressed up as responsiveness.

This is a leadership problem specifically, and it cannot be delegated. A coordinator can run a queue. Only a leader can hold a line. The hard part of managing demand is not tracking requests. It is telling a powerful person that their request is not the most important thing the team will do this month, and making that answer stick. The moment prioritization requires saying no to someone who outranks you, it stops being an administrative task and becomes an act of leadership. The teams that drown are almost never the ones that lacked a request form. They are the ones whose leader could not, or would not, hold the line the form was supposed to protect.

Prioritization starts with a defensible basis. What you need is a small set of questions you consistently apply to every request, out loud. Does this advance the strategy the organization already agreed to, or is it someone's pet project? How much value is at stake, in terms the business would recognize? What will it cost in the team's scarcest capacity? And what is the cost of waiting, which is not the same as the cost of the work? A regulatory deadline and a nice-to-have report can require the same effort but sit worlds apart in terms of the cost of delay.

The specific questions matter less than the fact that you apply them the same way every time and can explain your reasoning. Transparency is the real tool here. When the basis for prioritization is visible, a no stops feeling like a personal rejection and starts looking like a shared constraint. People can argue with a decision. They cannot argue with math they can see, at least not for long, and the argument they do have is a productive one about priorities rather than a resentful one about favoritism.

Which brings us to the skill most data leaders are worst at: saying no. The instinct is to avoid the word, to say yes and quietly let the work sit, or to say a flat no and absorb the resentment. Both are failures. The better move is to never say no in isolation. Say what the yes would cost. "Yes, we can start that in two weeks. To do it, I would pause the demand forecasting model the COO is waiting on. Which of those matters more to the two of you right now?" You have not refused. You have made the trade visible and handed the decision back to the people with the authority to make it. This is the translation discipline from the stakeholder chapter coming up, applied to your own capacity. Your job is not to block the request; it is to convert an invisible constraint into a choice the business can see and own.

The hardest version of this is upward, with the executive who sends requests by text at nine at night and expects them handled by morning. At Legacy, that executive is the CEO. Letting that pattern stand teaches the whole organization that the way to get data work done is to go around the process, which destroys the process. Resetting it is uncomfortable and unavoidable, and it is the managing-up work (discussed more in the stakeholder chapter) in its most concrete form: you are not refusing your leader; you are showing them that their informal request just jumped ahead of the committed work their own leadership team prioritized, and asking whether that is what they intend.

None of this holds if the team is planned to the last hour. A data organization running at 100% capacity cannot absorb urgent, real requests, so every genuine emergency becomes a crisis, and every crisis breaks something else. Protecting a margin of unallocated capacity is not slack in the lazy sense. It is the reserve that lets you say yes to the thing that matters without detonating three commitments to do it. The data engineering practice of holding 20% to 30% of capacity for operational work is the same principle applied to the whole function. Protecting that margin is also how you protect your people, who cannot do their best work while drowning, and a leader who lets the team drown to look responsive has chosen the wrong loyalty.

Managing demand well is not a form or a tool. The form is the easy part, and you will build it; the analytics request intake process later in this chapter is the machinery, a single front door that captures what decision a request supports and when it is needed. The discipline is the hard part, and it is yours. The mechanism can route the work, but only you can hold the line when someone powerful pushes against it, and holding that line, week after week, is what separates a data function that intentionally sets its priorities from one that is perpetually managed by the last person who called.

The Five Steps to Process Development

Building a new process or redesigning an existing one follows a consistent pattern drawn from Lean, Six Sigma, and Business Process Management.

Step 1: Identify the Need

A process improvement effort should begin when there is a specific, observable problem. The signals are usually unmistakable. Delays and backlogs indicating work is piling up somewhere, high error rates suggesting the process is not producing consistent outputs, stakeholder complaints about response times or accuracy, and employee frustration that is really friction with broken workflows.

A useful way to surface process problems is through structured scenario analysis. Consider what happens when an analyst delivers an analysis to a senior business leader with an incorrect conclusion. The immediate reaction in most organizations is to assign blame. The more productive approach is to ask, "Is this a process problem?" Almost certainly yes. Yes, the analyst made the mistake, but that mistake was not caught because the organization had no code review process, no peer validation step before high-stakes analyses reach senior leadership, and no automated testing that would have caught the error before it traveled downstream. The incident is the symptom. The missing process is the disease.

Most mistakes are process problems, and process problems are leadership problems.

Step 2: Document the Existing Process

Before designing a better process, you need an accurate picture of what is happening today, not what the documentation says should happen. There is almost always a gap between the nominal process and the actual one, which has workarounds, shortcuts, and informal hand-offs that developed because the nominal process was insufficient or overly complex for real-world conditions.

Documentation methods include stakeholder interviews to capture what people say they do and where it breaks down; process observation to capture what people do; document review to understand what someone once believed the process should be; and key performance indicators for the existing process to establish the baseline for any redesign. Without a baseline, you cannot measure whether the redesigned process is better.

Process visualization tools translate what you learn into a shareable artifact. Swimlane diagrams showing who does what and when are the most practical format for most data organization processes. A RACI matrix assigns each step or decision to one of four designations for each role involved. A process without a RACI is one without clear ownership, and it will be inconsistently executed.

Step 3: Design the New Process

Good process design is as much a facilitation exercise as a technical one. The people who will run the process should be central to its design. Start by defining the process objective in concrete, measurable terms. From the objective, build a process map that is detailed enough to produce consistent behavior across different people, but not so detailed as to prescribe every micro-decision. The test is whether a competent new team member could execute this process correctly from the documentation alone.

Four design choices require explicit attention. There are roles and responsibilities (who is responsible, accountable, consulted, informed at each step); tools and systems (which systems the process will use, where work will be tracked); decision criteria (what determines which path is taken at every fork, documented specifically enough that "use judgment" is not the answer); and automation (what parts of the process can be systematically automated to reduce error and enforce compliance). Test the design before committing to it by walking it through with the people who will execute it.

Step 4: Implement the New Process

Implementation asks people to change how they work. Change is uncomfortable. Effective implementation communicates the change with a clear "why" that connects to what it means for the people executing it; provides training that goes beyond distributing documentation; pilots before full rollout (four to six weeks across a realistic cross-section of use cases, not one week in ideal conditions); and builds a reinforcement architecture that embeds the process into tooling defaults, performance expectations, and leadership behavior. The Prosci ADKAR model provides a useful lens at the individual level: Awareness, Desire, Knowledge, Ability, and Reinforcement. Kotter's 8-step model addresses the organizational level. Both are covered in depth in Part 3.[48]

Step 5: Continuous Feedback and Improvement

A deployed process that is not monitored will gradually diverge from what the organization needs. Build feedback mechanisms into the process itself. Satisfaction surveys at the conclusion of significant outputs, regular retrospectives, and a process suggestion system that signals to the team that their operational experience is valued.

Process performance metrics should include cycle time, throughput, first-pass yield, exception rate, and SLA compliance. A process worth improving shows increasing cycle time or declining first-pass yield but still produces correct outputs when

---

48 **Developing Processes:** Jeff Hiatt, ADKAR: A Model for Change in Business, Government, and Our Community (Loveland, CO: Prosci Learning Center Publications, 2006); John P. Kotter, Leading Change (Boston: Harvard Business School Press, 1996).

executed carefully. A process worth retiring has an exception rate of 25-30%, is routinely worked around, or was designed for a technology stack or organizational structure that no longer exists.

These five steps are a framework for thinking about process development, not a checklist to run in full for every process on your team. A change to how customer financial data gets validated before it reaches a model deserves all five steps, in order, done carefully. A tweak to which day the team sends its weekly status update does not, and forcing it through the same five-step rigor is its own kind of failure, the "overly complex, with more steps and approvals than the outcome warrants" problem named earlier in this chapter, just self-inflicted this time instead of inherited. The right question before changing anything is not whether you completed all five steps. It is whether you thought about them, even briefly. For a small process, that thinking might take five minutes and never leave your own head. For a process that touches how the business makes decisions, it should take real time and involve the people who will run it. Match the rigor to the stakes, not to the existence of the framework.

Project Management Methodologies for Data Work

How to manage the execution of processes is a closely related question. Three methodologies are most commonly used in data organizations, and the right choice depends on the type of work being managed.

Waterfall is a sequential approach in which each phase must be completed before the next begins: Requirements, design, development, testing, deployment. Scope is fixed upfront, documentation is extensive, and changes mid-project are expensive. Waterfall fits a narrower set of data situations than its historical dominance would suggest: large-scale data platform migrations where architecture decisions carry multi-year consequences, regulatory reporting builds with legally mandated deliverables, and vendor-led implementations. The failure mode that makes Waterfall a poor choice for most data work is the assumption that requirements can be fully specified before any artifact exists for stakeholders to react to. In analytics and data science work, users almost universally discover what they need by seeing something that is not quite right. That discovery process requires iteration.

Agile, implemented through Scrum or Kanban, breaks work into short cycles, delivers working artifacts at the end of each cycle, and incorporates stakeholder feedback before the next begins. Scrum organizes work into time-boxed sprints with planning, daily stand-ups, a sprint review, and a retrospective. It fits data work well when the output is iterative and demonstrable: a dashboard suite, a data product, a predictive model. Kanban organizes work in a continuous flow rather than fixed sprints, with the core discipline of limiting work in progress to prevent multitasking, which degrades quality and throughput. Kanban fits operational and continuous work well, pipeline support, ad hoc analytics requests, and data quality remediation. In practice, most mature data teams use Scrum and Kanban together, depending on the function and size of the work: Scrum for project and product work, and Kanban for operational support.

DataOps applies Agile project management, DevOps engineering practices, and Lean quality principles specifically to data work. The core insight is that data pipelines, models, and analytical products should be developed and operated with the same engineering rigor that software teams apply to application code. In practice, DataOps manifests as version control for all transformation code and orchestration logic; automated testing at every pipeline stage covering schema, freshness, uniqueness, and value constraints; CI/CD pipelines that promote changes through development, staging, and production environments without manual deployment; observability tools that continuously monitor data for anomalies; and service-level objectives for data products that translate reliability into measurable, accountable commitments.

What methodology fits which data function? BI and analytics work fits iterative approaches. Scrum for teams with defined scope and stakeholders who can commit to sprint reviews; Kanban for earlier-stage teams where priorities shift quickly. Data engineering follows a hybrid sprint-based planning model for new pipeline development, with 20% to 30% capacity reserved for operational support. That reserved capacity is an honest accounting of what production engineering requires, not a planning failure. Data governance fits program management rather than sprints. It is an operating model with a steering committee and quarterly review cadence, not a project with a completion date.

The Seven Critical Processes

Strategy gets organizations to the starting line. Process keeps them on the field. There are seven processes that data leaders discover they need and build too late, usually after an incident has forced the conversation.

Data incident response includes severity classification, automated detection, on-call rotation, communication protocol, mitigation workflow, and a blameless post-mortem. The post-mortem is the most important element. An organization that holds blameless post-mortems and acts on their findings gets measurably better over time. One that assigns blame produces teams that conceal problems rather than surfacing them.

Data quality remediation runs continuously, catching issues before they become incidents. Automated tests against the data estate run on a defined schedule, failures route to the appropriate owner, and resolution is tracked through to completion with ownership and resolution SLAs assigned.

Analytics request intake provides a single entry point that captures the decision the request will support, when it is needed, and who the decision-maker is. Without it, analytics teams are managed by whoever is loudest or most senior. With it, work is prioritized by business value and committed delivery dates are set based on capacity rather than pressure.

New data source onboarding addresses every consideration introduced by a new source: source assessment, legal and data protection review, security review, ingestion design, catalog registration, access policy assignment, data quality test definition, SLA agreement, and production cutover with monitoring enabled. Without it, new sources accumulate without documentation, ownership, or tests.

Model deployment covers the full transition from notebook to production, model registration, feature validation, automated training and evaluation pipelines, staging deployment, production monitoring for drift and accuracy, retraining triggers, and versioned rollback capability. Without it, a business user discovers degraded model performance rather than the data team.

Data access requests route through a catalog or portal, automatically identify the data owner, apply a consistent policy-based evaluation, provision access with explicit scope limits, and maintain an audit trail for compliance review. Modern best practice applies least-privilege by default, time-bounded grants, and regular access recertification for both human and non-human (pipeline and AI agent) identities.

Definition and metric change management requires any proposed change to a key business definition to go through a governance channel. This includes impact analysis across all dashboards, models, and reports that reference the definition; review and approval from the data owner and affected stakeholders; versioned implementation in the semantic layer; consumer communication with a transition period; and retirement of the old definition on a defined date. Skipping this process leads to the "we have three different numbers for revenue" problem, which drives more business distrust of data than almost any other single cause.

Further Reading

Foundational works for going deeper on this topic:

Atomic Habits, by James Clear, the source of this chapter's opening idea: that goals rarely separate winners from everyone else chasing the same ones; systems do.

The Data Product Playbook, by Willem Koenders, a concrete look at operating models and adoption for data work, including the same Kotter change model referenced elsewhere in this book.

Scrum: The Art of Doing Twice the Work in Half the Time, by Jeff Sutherland, from Scrum's co-creator, the clearest explanation of why the methodology works and where it came from.

Legacy Paper and Supply: Developing Processes

The data strategy is approved, the roadmap is funded, and the team is executing. The branch dashboard is live, the forecasting model is in development, and the customer intelligence application is scoped. Senior leadership is engaged in a way they have never been before. And with that engagement comes something nobody fully prepared for: demand.

More requests. More stakeholders. More source systems coming online. More people who now know the data team exists and have opinions about what it should be building next. The team that was adequate to deliver three focused IDS commitments is not automatically equipped to operate as a mature data organization. That gap is a process gap, and it surfaces in three distinct ways within the first few months of TDS execution.

The first appears when a change is made to the order management platform without anyone notifying the data team. A new product categorization scheme was implemented as part of a system update, altering how product categories are classified going back three months. Nobody told the data team because nobody had a process for telling them. The branch dashboard, which has been running reliably for two months, now shows category trends inconsistent with historical data that predates the change. Two business leaders have already made decisions based on those trends. The data team learns when a regional director calls to ask why her paper category numbers differ from what she heard in a branch manager meeting.

This incident produces two critical processes. The first is a source system change management protocol: any change to a system that could affect data structure, classification, or availability must be communicated to the data organization before deployment, with a minimum two-week lead time. The conversation with the head of IT is initially uncomfortable because it adds a step to an established change process. You frame it instead as risk management, since an unannounced schema change can silently corrupt outputs that business leaders use to make decisions, and the liability for those decisions flows back to the data team. That framing lands. The second process is automated data quality monitoring across every production table: freshness checks, volume anomaly detection, and consistency checks running on a schedule with alerts when something unexpected appears.

The second gap surfaces as the team's reputation grows. Requests begin arriving from every direction and through every channel: email to individual team members, messages through the CEO's assistant, conversations at company all-hands, direct texts to you. Within a month, the team is spread across nine partially completed requests, none moving quickly enough to satisfy anyone, with team members context-switching so frequently that nothing is getting done well.

Legacy implements a formal intake and prioritization process. All requests enter through a single form. You triage the queue every other week with the COO and VP of Sales, setting committed delivery dates based on capacity rather than pressure and communicating those dates back to requesters. Work that arrives outside the form is acknowledged but not prioritized ahead of committed work. Establishing this norm requires a direct conversation with the CEO, who initially sends requests informally, expecting an immediate response. That conversation is worth having. Within six weeks, the team is delivering more, not less, because focused execution on one thing at a time outperforms fragmented effort across many.

The third gap emerges as the team begins deploying models and AI applications. The demand forecasting model has been validated and is ready for production. The question is what production means for a machine learning model. How does it get deployed, how do you monitor whether it continues to perform, who is responsible for retraining it when accuracy degrades, and what happens if it produces a forecast that leads to a costly procurement decision that turns out to be wrong? Without answers, a model that performs well in development is not a model the business can rely on.

Legacy builds a model governance and MLOps process that covers the full model lifecycle, including registration before deployment with documentation of training data, validation results, and known limitations; staging review by the relevant business team before going live; a monitoring dashboard that tracks accuracy against actuals on a defined schedule; a retraining trigger when performance falls below a defined threshold; and a clear escalation path when a model is wrong in a consequential way. This last piece is not glamorous. It is the process that determines whether the business continues to trust AI outputs after the first significant error, or stops trusting them entirely.

These three processes did not exist before the team needed them. None were anticipated in the strategy document. All emerged from specific operational realities that only become visible once the organization is executing at scale. That is the nature of process development in a growing data organization. You cannot design every process in advance, but you can build the habit of converting every recurring problem into a documented, owned, repeatable solution. The teams that do this consistently are the ones that scale.

The next chapter covers hiring data talent. The people decisions that determine whether the strategy and processes you have built can be executed.

TEN

Hiring Data Talent

You have a strategy. You have processes. Now you need people.

The strategy defines the direction. The processes define how work gets done reliably. The people are what make it happen.

Hire well, and everything else becomes easier.
Hire poorly, and everything else becomes harder.

Data talent is scarce at the senior and specialized levels. The skills required change faster than most educational systems can track. Compensation expectations are high. The people you need most are often already employed, receiving outreach from multiple organizations simultaneously. And once you find them, hire them, and get them productive, keeping them requires sustained attention and investment.

Build, Buy, or Borrow Talent

The most important talent question you face is not how to hire. It is whether to hire at all.

Every data capability gap can be addressed through one of three approaches. You can build it by developing the capability internally with training, upskilling, or redeploying existing employees. You can buy it by hiring externally to bring in the capability as a permanent employee. Or you can borrow it by using contractors, consultants, or staffing partners to access the capability on a temporary or project basis.

Building is the right choice when the capability is strategically core, when a realistic development path exists within your training budget and timeline, or when retention matters more than speed. Research from Wharton and SHRM finds that internally promoted employees tend to outperform external hires during their first two years and cost meaningfully less all-in. Internal moves measurably reduce attrition intent, a pattern the retention data below makes concrete. An analyst who has spent two years understanding your company's data quirks, business rules, and organizational dynamics is often more valuable than an external hire with stronger technical credentials who needs a year to learn the terrain.

Buying is the right choice when internal capability does not exist or cannot be built in a reasonable timeframe, when urgency is high, or when the role requires an outside perspective that internal talent cannot provide. The tradeoffs are real: external hires cost 18 to 35% more in direct costs, typically take three to six months to reach full productivity, and leave at higher rates than internally developed talent.

Borrowing is the right choice for time-bounded needs, a one-time platform migration, a governance framework buildout requiring specialized expertise, a bridge engagement while a permanent search is underway, or a specific technical project that does not justify a permanent hire. For smaller organizations in the early stages of data maturity, bringing in senior consulting expertise while building junior talent permanently is often the most capital-efficient approach.

If the capability is strategically core and the timeline permits, build. If the capability is not present internally and urgency is real, buy. If the need is time-bounded or specialized, borrow. Most mature data organizations run all three simultaneously.

Identifying Necessary Skillsets

The starting point for any hiring decision is the data strategy, not the job description. Your strategy defines the outcomes you aim to produce and the capabilities you need to achieve them. Translating that into a hiring plan requires four questions: What skillsets do you need to accomplish your goals? What skillsets already exist in your organization? What are the gaps? And what is your budget?

Data talent at the senior and AI-specialized levels commands significant compensation. In 2025 and 2026, data engineering roles carry median compensation in the $130,000 to $150,000 range, with modern-stack specialists earning more. AI engineers with LLM and RAG experience command salaries of $200,000 or more at many organizations. ML engineers typically sit in the $165,000 to $200,000 range. Data scientists range from $120,000 to $160,000 depending on seniority. Data analysts range from $80,000 to $120,000, though that range is compressing at the junior end as AI tools reduce demand for routine analytical work. These are directional figures; actual compensation depends heavily on geography, industry, and company size. Triangulate across at least three benchmarking sources rather than relying on any single estimate.

The data talent market is bifurcated. At the senior, AI-specialized, and platform-engineering levels, scarcity is severe. Robert Half's 2026 technology hiring research found that AI, machine learning, and data science are the hardest skills to find, and only 7% of technology hiring managers feel confident they can fill their in-demand roles.[49] At the junior and generalist levels, there is a surplus in some markets, as AI tools automate routine analytical tasks and a wave of coding bootcamp graduates entered the

---

[49] **Hiring Data Talent:** Robert Half, 2026 Technology Hiring Managers and Skilled Talent Research Report (Robert Half, 2026).

market simultaneously. Your hiring strategy for a senior machine learning engineer and a junior analyst is fundamentally different.

Creating a Recruiting Strategy

The best candidates in data are often not browsing job boards out of desperation. They are receiving outreach from multiple organizations and making decisions based on what they know and believe about each company's data culture and technical environment before they ever talk to a recruiter.

Employer brand in data is built through visibility and credibility, including technical blog posts, conference presence, employee-generated content about the team's work, and honesty in recruiting conversations about what the environment looks like. Candidates who join with accurate expectations stay longer than those who were oversold.

Job postings attract active seekers. Targeted sourcing means going to find them. LinkedIn InMails that demonstrate you have read the candidate's profile (personalized messages have meaningfully higher response rates than templates), data-specific conferences like dbt Coalesce and Data Council, GitHub and Kaggle profiles to identify practitioners with demonstrated work product, and university partnerships for graduate recruiting.

Effective job descriptions for data roles are specific and honest, written for the candidate rather than the compliance department. They distinguish between required and preferred qualifications. They include a pay range: beyond the growing number of states where this is legally required, publishing ranges saves everyone's time and attracts candidates whose expectations align with reality.

Running the Interview Process

Before designing an interview process, internalize one thing. The best candidates in this field are evaluating you as much as you are evaluating them. A data engineer with strong modern-stack skills and a track record of delivering production-quality work has options. What they are looking for in an interview process is a signal about what it would be like to work there. Is the technical bar real? Do the people interviewing them know what good work looks like? Is the organization one where their skills will be used well or underutilized? A disorganized interview process that asks irrelevant questions or that takes six weeks and five rounds sends a clear signal before the offer letter arrives. So does one that is crisp, technically serious, respectful of the candidate's time, and honest about what the role involves.

There is a growing trend toward adding more and more interview stages. It does not produce better hiring decisions. It produces candidate drop-off, extended time-to-hire, and a signal that the organization does not respect the candidate's time. With proper preparation and structured evaluation criteria, two to three well-designed interviews will surface what you need to know about most candidates.

A typical interview sequence for data roles includes an initial screen to verify basic fit and alignment on expectations; a technical evaluation that reflects the actual work of the role (SQL and analytical reasoning for data analysts, pipeline design and debugging for data engineers, modeling and validation approaches for data scientists); a behavioral interview that probes past experience through structured questions about how the candidate has operated in relevant contexts; and a final conversation with additional team members focused on mutual fit. Time-limiting take-home assignments to three to four hours and responding to every candidate within five business days of each stage meaningfully improve completion rates.

A word on gimmicks. Abstract puzzle questions, whiteboard algorithm challenges, and "How many windows are in New York City?" questions do not predict job performance. Google ran its own internal analysis and confirmed this before banning them entirely. What brainteasers measure is whether the candidate has encountered that type of question before, not how they think or how they will perform in the role. Technical evaluations are worth using, but only when they reflect the actual work, a realistic pipeline debugging exercise for a data engineer, or a SQL and analytical reasoning problem for an analyst. The test for any evaluation is simple: Does this exercise tell me something about how well this person will step into this role, do the work, and be a great teammate? If the honest answer is no, cut it.

What to Look for in Candidates

Skill and experience match is the starting point. Does the candidate have the technical capabilities the role requires, and is their experience applied rather than merely conceptual? Cultural fit matters, but it deserves careful definition. It should mean alignment with how the team approaches its work, rigor, transparency, intellectual honesty, and genuine collaboration across technical and business lines. It should not mean someone who reminds the interviewer of themselves. When cultural fit becomes a mechanism for homogeneity, it becomes a source of bias.

The strongest data professionals are also drawn to genuine difficulty. They want to work on problems that are not already solved, on teams where the work is technically serious and the stakes are real. When you are interviewing someone exceptional, they are assessing whether your organization offers that. A candidate who asks hard questions about your data infrastructure, your governance maturity, your approach to model deployment, or what the most difficult analytical problem the team has faced recently is not being presumptuous. They are doing exactly what you would want a rigorous, motivated data professional to do. Answering those questions honestly, including the ones that reveal gaps, will attract better people than the one who oversells the environment. The candidate you want is the one who is excited by the challenge despite the gaps.

Potential and learning agility are particularly important in data and AI roles because the technology changes fast enough that today's skill set depreciates within two to three years. Decades of industrial-organizational psychology research, including meta-analyses by Schmidt and Hunter, found that years of experience is one of the worst predictors of job performance. Structured interviews, work samples, and cognitive ability all predict better. A candidate with two years of experience building RAG systems may be better prepared for a 2026 ML engineering role than a candidate with five years of pre-generative-AI machine learning experience.

This has a direct implication for what you screen for. As AI absorbs more of the routine technical execution, such as writing a first draft of code, generating a baseline model, or summarizing a dataset, the differentiator between a good hire and a great one shifts. Two candidates with comparable technical proficiency are no longer distinguished primarily by who codes faster or knows more frameworks. They are distinguished by who asks better questions about the business problem, who can explain a tradeoff to a skeptical stakeholder, and who knows when the AI-generated answer is subtly wrong. This does not mean technical skill stops mattering. It means technical competence increasingly functions as a threshold you have to clear rather than the primary axis you hire on. Above that threshold, judgment, communication, and the ability to connect technical work to a business outcome are what separate candidates.

The strongest data organizations are built from people who came to the field through different paths: engineers who retrained, analysts who went deep into machine learning, domain experts who learned to work with data, and practitioners who built skills outside formal education. Sourcing from diverse channels, writing job descriptions that do not unnecessarily narrow the pipeline, and using structured interviews with consistent rubrics all help ensure the process is evaluating relevant capability rather than filtering for a narrow profile of what a data professional is supposed to look like on paper.

Offers and Onboarding

Extend the offer personally via phone or video call before the formal letter arrives. Congratulate the candidate and articulate specifically why they are the right choice. State all terms clearly: title, base salary, bonus, equity (if applicable), and start date. A decision window of five to seven days is standard. Pressure tactics damage the employer brand and lead to forced acceptances that become early exits.

Compensation decisions should be anchored to a defensible internal band informed by current market data and consistent across similar employees. Asking candidates what they currently make is illegal in over twenty states, and structuring offers around individual negotiating leverage rather than consistent internal bands creates both legal risk and employee relations problems.

A well-structured onboarding process is one of the highest-return investments you can make. Set up workstations, accounts, and access before the first day so time is spent meeting people and learning the work, not waiting for a laptop to be provisioned. In the first week, orient the new hire to the organization, the data function's role within it, and the team. In the first month, assign a small-scoped project that lets them learn the codebase and working practices while producing something real. Provide a buddy who can answer the questions that are too small for a formal meeting but too important to go unanswered. Conduct a thirty-day check-in to surface early concerns before they calcify. True onboarding takes three to six months for most data professionals; the attention that characterized the early weeks cannot fade as the initial novelty wears off.

Further Reading

Foundational works for going deeper on this topic:

Who: The A Method for Hiring, by Geoff Smart and Randy Street, a structured, repeatable approach to interviewing that reduces the guesswork this chapter warns against.

Work Rules!, by Laszlo Bock, Google's former head of People Operations, on what the data says about hiring, developing, and keeping talent.

Legacy Paper and Supply: Hiring Data Talent

The data strategy has been approved, and the TDS use case portfolio includes 23 documented initiatives. Now comes the question that determines whether any of it happens: "Do you have the right people to execute?"

The answer, when you are honest about it, is not yet. But the first step is not posting a job. It is looking at what you already have.

Building the IDS Team

Legacy already has one data professional, a data analyst who has been producing manual reports for years. She knows the business deeply, understands where the data quirks are, and has been increasingly frustrated by the lack of tools and infrastructure to do more sophisticated work. A conversation in your first week reveals something important. She wants to move toward data engineering and architecture. Not just because the business needs it, but because her intellectual interests are pulling her there.

Rather than hiring around her, you invest in her. dbt training, direct exposure to the platform work the incoming data engineer will be doing, and a clear development path toward an analytics engineering role. She carries both roles simultaneously in the near term, continuing to produce the analytical work the business depends on while building the engineering skills she needs. That transition plan has a defined horizon, and she is in it by choice. She will eventually be one of the most valuable people on the team, an engineer who understands the business problems the data is supposed to solve, because she spent years solving them herself.

The first external hire is a full-time data engineer. The data platform is the foundation on which every use case in the portfolio depends, and foundational infrastructure needs a permanent owner from day one. The recruiting pitch is honest and specific. Building from scratch, real ownership of the platform, visibility to the executive team in a way that engineers at larger organizations rarely have. For the right candidate at the right career stage, that pitch is compelling. The interview process is scoped to three stages: a recruiter screen, a 90-minute technical interview with structured rubrics, and a final conversation focused not on technical skills but on how the candidate thinks about stakeholder relationships and communicates with non-technical audiences. Total elapsed time from first outreach to offer is three weeks.

By the end of the IDS, the team is four people: you, the analytics engineer in transition, the data engineer, and a data scientist hired at month four once the bronze and silver layers are in place and there is clean enough data to begin feature engineering for the forecasting model. Small, but capable of delivering on all three use cases with the right sequencing and support.

Building the TDS Team

Before describing the TDS team build, a caveat is needed. The compensation figures and role sequences below are realistic approximations, not prescriptions. Every organization has different use cases, skill sets, technical debt, regulatory exposure, and budget realities. What Legacy's hiring journey illustrates is a way of thinking. Start with the use cases the business needs to deliver, identify the bottlenecks slowing delivery, and use that analysis to prioritize which roles to hire, in what order, and whether they should be permanent or contracted. The specific answers will differ everywhere. The questions should be the same.

The TDS approval includes a $1.5 million budget. After cloud infrastructure, tooling, and overhead, roughly $1.1 million is available for people. Five permanent hires and two time-bound contractors over an 18-month period.

The first TDS hire is a data architect at $145,000. This is the role most early-stage data organizations skip and most mature ones wish they had not. The TDS has twenty-three use cases that will generate significant modeling and platform complexity. Without an architect designing the data models that underpin it all, the engineering team builds on top of whatever seemed reasonable at the time, and the accumulated technical debt becomes expensive to unwind. The architect works closely with the data engineer to formalize the conceptual model sketched in the architecture chapter, extend it across the full TDS portfolio, and establish the design standards that future engineers and data scientists will work within.

The second hire is a second full-time data engineer at $140,000. By month six of TDS execution, the platform build is generating more work than one engineer can absorb. Two contractors are also brought on for six-month engagements at $85,000 each, for targeted surge capacity for specific build work, including standing up the feature store, building data infrastructure for the AI application, and accelerating source system integrations. When the surge work is complete, the contractor engagements end. The permanent engineers own what was built.

The third permanent hire is a data governance and management lead at $125,000, a combined role by design. At Legacy's scale, the governance and management functions are sufficiently intertwined that splitting them into two separate roles is premature. The right person can design and implement a governance framework, establish data ownership and stewardship processes, and manage operational data quality and master data work to keep the platform trustworthy. By the time this hire joins, the team has been managing governance informally for over a year and the debt is visible. This role takes that work off the engineering team's plate.

The fourth hire is a data analyst with BI proficiency at $95,000. The analytics engineer has fully transitioned into her engineering role. She is no longer building dashboards or answering ad-hoc questions. She is building data models and pipeline architecture.

That transition is exactly what both she and the business need. But it creates an analytical gap: branch managers are submitting dashboard requests nobody is picking up, and the data scientist is being pulled from modeling work to answer questions a good analyst could handle. This hire fills that gap.

The fifth hire is a second data analyst at $85,000. As the TDS portfolio expands and more business leaders engage with the data organization, analytical demand grows faster than one analyst can absorb. The second hire supports a different set of business units and use cases, provides the team with redundancy on critical reporting workflows, and creates capacity for both analysts to go deeper into their respective domains rather than being perpetually reactive.

At full TDS build-out, Legacy's data organization includes you, an analytics engineer advancing toward architecture, two full-time data engineers, a data architect, a data scientist, a data governance and management lead, and two data analysts. Nine people, plus contractor surge capacity as needed. A team capable of executing a meaningful TDS at a company of Legacy's size, with enough specialization to go deep on each function and enough breadth to collaborate across them.

This team cannot complete all twenty-three TDS use cases in a year, and it was never meant to. The roadmap gives business leaders visibility into where their initiatives sit and a realistic picture of when to expect delivery. It also establishes the structure for the conversations that occur constantly throughout TDS execution. Reprioritization occurs as the business changes: new use cases are introduced as opportunities emerge and old use cases are deprioritized as circumstances evolve. A data organization with a documented, visible roadmap can have those conversations productively. One without it is constantly defending its choices and rebuilding trust it should have earned by being transparent from the start.

The work of building this team does not end when the last hire is made. It is a continuous cycle of assessing the strategy, identifying the capability gaps, deciding what to build, buy, or borrow, hiring deliberately, onboarding well, developing relentlessly, and creating the conditions under which the people hired for what they can do today become the people who can do what the organization needs tomorrow. The analytics engineer who started as a manual reporting analyst is the clearest proof of that principle. She became an engineer because you saw where she wanted to go, created the conditions for her to get there, and gave her the time and the work to develop. That is what data leadership looks like when it is working.

This chapter closes Part 2. You now have a strategy, processes, and a team. Part 3 covers the work of leading that team and the organization around it. The human dimensions of data leadership that no technical foundation can substitute for.

Part III

Leading Data Organizations

Parts 1 and 2 were about understanding data organizations and building them. You increased your understanding of how data organizations work, what each function does, and why the technical and governance foundations matter. Then you built the organization itself, a strategy grounded in business outcomes, processes that make execution repeatable, and a team capable of carrying the work forward.

Part 3 is even harder. Executing.

Leading is different from building. Building has a satisfying quality: you make decisions, allocate resources, and construct things. You can see the progress. Leading is less visible and more continuous. It is the daily practice of setting direction when the direction is unclear, developing people who may eventually leave you, navigating organizational politics that no framework fully prepares you for, and holding the team together when the work is difficult and the business is impatient.

This module covers the human side of running a data organization: how to lead your team, manage relationships with the stakeholders on whom your work depends, navigate organizational change, grow the function, and measure and communicate its value. These are the skills that separate data leaders who build something lasting from those who build something impressive that does not survive their departure.

ELEVEN

Leading Data Talent

There is a quiet crisis in data leadership that nobody talks about enough. Data organizations are disproportionately led by people who were never trained to lead. They were trained to analyze, engineer, model, and govern. They were excellent at the work, which is exactly why they were promoted. Then they arrived in leadership roles and discovered that the skills that made them excellent individual contributors are largely irrelevant to the ones they now need. The best SQL query in the world will not help you give difficult feedback to a senior engineer who is underperforming. A beautifully optimized pipeline will not resolve a conflict between two analysts who cannot work together.

The people you lead are the job. Everything else, including the models, the pipelines, and the dashboards, is what the job produces once you get the people part right.

As I mentioned in the preface, my first leadership experience was in the Army's Old Guard, a ceremonial unit that prides itself on discipline. The mission itself was precision: honor formations, guard duty, moments where the entire point was exact, unwavering execution rather than judgment. I once told a soldier to wait in a spot while I handled something else, got pulled into other priorities, and returned several hours later to find him exactly where I had left him. He had not moved. My next leadership experience was a team of unionized customer service agents at a major airline, which ran on some very different logic. There was no order that commanded compliance on its own. You earned it through mutual respect and trust, built person by person, or you got none at all.

Data leadership turned out to be neither of those extremes. The people I was leading were highly skilled, deeply motivated by their craft, and had no shortage of options if they did not feel their work was valued. It clicked for me when I stopped thinking about it as leading soldiers or employees and started thinking about it as coaching professional athletes. Think about how the Golden State Warriors use Steph Curry. Nobody tells him when to shoot. The coaching staff builds a system, an offense designed around movement, spacing, and trust, in which his skills have room to operate at their highest level. The shot happens because the system created the conditions for it. Leading data professionals works the same way. You are not managing people who need to be told exactly what to do. You are creating the vision, systems, clarity, psychological safety, and organizational conditions in which highly skilled people can do their best work. Get that right, and the results will follow.

Get it wrong, and the cost is not abstract. People leave bad managers, not companies. A talented data scientist does not usually quit because the mission statement stopped resonating. She quits because she stopped being coached, stopped being heard, or watched her leader tolerate something that should not have been tolerated, and decided her judgment and her time were worth more somewhere else. Every skill this chapter covers, including the conversations, the feedback, and the standards you hold, is not management theory for its own sake. It is the difference between keeping the people this book has spent its previous chapters teaching you to hire, and losing them to someone who leads better.

The Individual Contributor to Leader Transition

This is the section most books on data leadership skip, and it is the one that matters most for the largest number of people reading this book.

The transition from individual contributor to leader is not a small adjustment. It is a fundamental redefinition of what your job is and where your value comes from. As an individual contributor, your output is what you produce, including the analysis you complete, the model you build, the pipeline you deploy. As a leader, your output is what your team produces. Your value is indirect and often invisible. You spent a week coaching a junior analyst through a difficult methodology problem, and the analyst received credit for the output, as they should. But you provided the coaching, and it was what made the output possible.

Common failure patterns to watch for include reverting to IC work under stress, because it is faster and more comfortable than delegating; pacesetting as a default style, which demoralizes junior members who cannot match the pace and makes the leader the ceiling of what the team can aspire to; avoiding people problems because they are harder than data problems; and confusing technical disagreement with performance issues. When a team member makes a technical choice you would not have made, the first question is not "Is this a performance issue?" The first question is "Did they have a good rationale?" Enforcing personal technical preferences as if they were objective requirements is one of the fastest ways to signal to skilled people that their judgment is not trusted.

Leadership Styles and When to Use Them

Goleman's 2000 HBR framework of six leadership styles[50] provides a useful vocabulary for thinking about how leadership

[50] Daniel Goleman, "Leadership That Gets Results," Harvard Business Review, March–April 2000.

behavior affects team climate. It deserves an honest caveat. The original dataset was not published in a peer-reviewed journal in a form that allows independent replication, and subsequent studies have produced variable results depending on organizational context. Treat it as diagnostic vocabulary, not a predictive model.

Commanding (do what I tell you) belongs in genuine crises requiring immediate action; used routinely, it creates fear and suppresses honest feedback. **Visionary** (come with me) has the most strongly positive climate impact of the six; most data leaders underuse it because it requires comfort with abstraction. **Affiliative** (people come first) heals rifts and builds trust, but overuse without accountability produces warmth without results. **Democratic** (What do you think?) belongs when you need input to make a good decision, but using it when the decision is already made is dishonest. **Pacesetting** (do as I do, now) works only with highly competent, motivated teams; the most common misuse is technically excellent data leaders who continue to perform at IC level and expect the team to match them. **Coaching** (try this) belongs with individuals who have development goals and are open to feedback, which in a healthy data team should be most of the team most of the time.

The most effective leaders are situationally aware and tailor their leadership styles to match.

They recognize what the moment requires and have enough range to respond appropriately.

Servant Leadership

Robert Greenleaf's servant leadership philosophy, introduced in his 1970 essay[51] and popularized for business audiences by Simon Sinek's *Leaders Eat Last*, holds that the leader serves the organization, the team, and the people in it rather than the reverse. The empirical research is strong. A 2024 review across two decades found favorable results in over 90% of studies measuring engagement, trust, innovation, and team performance.

For data teams, servant leadership pairs naturally with the autonomy and craftsmanship norms of skilled technical work. A leader who removes obstacles, advocates for resources, and trusts the team to make technical decisions within a clear strategic direction will outperform a leader who controls the work and manages by surveillance.

The limitation is that servant leadership can be misread as "the leader as service desk." Serving the team means giving them what they need to do their best work, including honest feedback, clear expectations, and protection from organizational dysfunction. It does not mean telling people what they want to hear or avoiding the decisions that only you can make.

---

[51] Robert K. Greenleaf, "The Servant as Leader" (Westfield, IN: Robert K. Greenleaf Center for Servant Leadership, 1970).

Vulnerability and What It Actually Means

Brené Brown's research at the University of Houston, particularly her books *Daring Greatly* (2012) and *Dare to Lead* (2018),[52] defines vulnerability as the willingness to show up and engage with uncertainty, risk, and emotional exposure without guarantees of the outcome. Her central argument for leadership is that courage requires vulnerability, and that leaders who operate from behind armor, projecting certainty, deflecting criticism, and never admitting doubt, build cultures of performance and fear rather than cultures of learning and honesty.

For data leaders, this shows up in concrete ways. Saying "I don't know the answer to that" in a meeting rather than bluffing. Acknowledging when a decision you made turned out to be wrong rather than rationalizing it. Asking your team for their honest assessment of an initiative before committing publicly to it. These small acts of intellectual honesty, repeated consistently, build something that cannot be manufactured any other way: a team that feels safe being honest with you.

The nuances matter. Brown is explicit that vulnerability is strategic and contextual, not cathartic or indiscriminate. There is a meaningful difference between telling your team you are

[52] Brené Brown, Daring Greatly: How the Courage to Be Vulnerable Transforms the Way We Live, Love, Parent, and Lead (New York: Gotham Books, 2012); Brené Brown, Dare to Lead: Brave Work. Tough Conversations. Whole Hearts. (New York: Random House, 2018).

uncertain about a technical direction and inviting their expertise, and unloading existential anxieties about the function's budget situation on a recently joined junior analyst. The first builds trust and invites contribution. The second creates fear and recruits the team into a problem they cannot solve. Vulnerability is not the same as oversharing, and power asymmetry matters. What is safe for a peer-to-peer conversation can be destabilizing when the person sharing it has formal authority over the people listening.

The test is purpose. Sharing uncertainty to invite expertise serves the team. Sharing anxiety to relieve your own discomfort burdens them.

Underneath all of it is humility, which may be the least discussed leadership trait in data. The field moves fast enough that some of what you know is already wrong, and you will spend your entire career working alongside people who know their specialty better than you do. Humility is what lets you say so out loud. It is an accurate read of what you know, what you do not, and who in the room knows better. Teams can tell the difference between a leader who performs certainty and one who is honest about their limits, and they give their best thinking to the second one.

Psychological Safety

Google's Project Aristotle studied 180 teams to find what distinguished high performers from low performers. They found that psychological safety, defined by Amy Edmondson as "a shared belief held by members of a team that the team is safe for interpersonal risk taking," predicted team performance more reliably than any other factor they measured.[53]

For data teams, psychological safety is not a nice-to-have. It is a prerequisite for the function to work honestly. An analyst who notices an anomaly in a key metric the CEO has been citing in board presentations needs to feel safe enough to surface it. A data scientist who does not understand why a model is behaving unexpectedly needs to feel safe saying "I don't know." In a psychologically unsafe team, both of those people bury the problem, and the organization suffers for it.

Specific leader behaviors that build psychological safety include framing the work as a learning problem, not an execution problem; acknowledging your own fallibility openly; modeling curiosity by asking genuine questions; responding productively to bad news; and rewarding the act of speaking up, not just the correctness of the concern.

This extends to pushback on your own decisions, not just uncertainty about the work. Your teams should also feel safe saying the priority you just set seems wrong, or that a deadline you

---

[53] **Leading Data Talent:** Amy C. Edmondson, "Psychological Safety and Learning Behavior in Work Teams," Administrative Science Quarterly 44, no. 2 (1999): 350–83; Charles Duhigg, "What Google Learned from Its Quest to Build the Perfect Team," New York Times Magazine, February 25, 2016, reporting on Google's Project Aristotle study of 180 teams.

committed to is unrealistic given what the team knows. Reward that pushback visibly, and especially when it turns out to be right, and especially in front of others, because a team learns far more from watching how you react the one time someone challenges you than from anything you say beforehand about wanting to be challenged. A leader who claims to welcome disagreement but visibly bristles the first time it happens has just taught the team the real rule, and no amount of stated policy said afterward undoes that lesson.

Important clarification. Psychological safety is not the absence of accountability. Edmondson's quadrant model places them on separate axes. The high-performing zone combines both. A team with high psychological safety and low standards is comfortable but unproductive. The goal is a team where people feel safe enough to be honest and accountable enough to care about the outcomes.[54]

Commander's Intent

Commander's Intent is a U.S. military doctrine term, and it is embedded in joint doctrine across every branch of service. Anyone who has served knows it. Before an operation, the commander articulates what success looks like and why the

---

54 Amy C. Edmondson, The Fearless Organization: Creating Psychological Safety in the Workplace for Learning, Innovation, and Growth (Hoboken, NJ: Wiley, 2018).

mission matters, then trusts subordinate commanders to achieve that end state using their own judgment when the plan encounters friction, which it always does. The specific how is left to the people closest to the situation. The what and the why belong to the commander. David Marquet's *Turn the Ship Around!* and Stephen Bungay's *The Art of Action* brought the concept to business audiences, and both are worth reading.

For data teams, the application is direct. Consider two ways to brief a data scientist:

"The VP wants a dashboard with customer acquisition cost, lifetime value, and churn rate by segment. Pull from the CRM and the revenue tables and build it in Tableau."

Versus:

"The VP is getting asked hard questions about which customer segments are worth acquiring and retaining. They don't have a clear picture of the economics. Can you help them understand where we're making money and where we're not?"

The first asks for execution of a specification. The second asks for problem-solving. The second might produce a dashboard, or a memo, or a conversation that reframes the question entirely. It also produces something else: a data scientist who is developing judgment and understands the business well enough to contribute to it rather than just execute tasks.

> *Tell your team the problem you are trying to solve and what success looks like, then get out of the way. The best data professionals will surprise you with their ingenuity when you give them room to be ingenious.*

One-on-Ones

The most important recurring meeting on your calendar is the one-on-one with each direct report. Done well, these meetings are the primary mechanism through which you develop people, understand what is actually happening on the team, and maintain the trust that makes everything else possible.

One-on-ones belong to the direct report, not the leader. The employee should own the agenda. The topics should be what they need, not what you want to check on. Status updates about active projects belong in stand-ups or async channels. The one-on-one is for development conversations, obstacles you can help remove, feedback in both directions, and the long-term relationship between the employee and their career at this organization. If your one-on-ones feel like status meetings, that is a design problem, and the fix starts with saying so explicitly: "This is your meeting. What's on your mind?"

Even the opening question matters more than it seems. I ask, "How's life?" instead of something like "How are you?" The difference sounds trivial but in my experience you get vastly different answers. "How are you?" invites a reflexive "fine, busy" and a fast pivot into whatever is on the agenda that they're working on. "How's life?" is intended to show a genuine interest in them as people and they tend to answer it that way. They'll share an upcoming move, a new relationship, a parent's health, a kid starting school. None of that is owed to you, and there should be no expectation for them to share it. But the analyst who mentions, almost in passing, that her mother has been sick is telling you something worth knowing as her leader, because it explains the distracted energy you might otherwise misread as a dip in commitment. You are not entitled to that information. She volunteered it when you ask a question that leaves room for it, and what you do with that knowledge (more patience that week, a lighter load, or simply understanding rather than acting) is a real part of the job.

Be on time. Joining five minutes late sends a message before you have said a word. Repeatedly moving the meeting to accommodate your schedule signals, regardless of intent, that other things matter more than this person does. Over time, that signal accumulates into a belief, and the belief affects what they are willing to bring to you.

The specific conversation that Russ Laraway recommends in *When They Win, You Win* is worth adopting as a practice: a single long-form "Career Conversation" that asks three questions. What experiences and choices in your life have made you who you are? What do you dream of doing in the long run? What do you need to develop in the next two years to move toward that? Run this conversation once a year per person. It takes 90 minutes and produces more retention-relevant information than any amount of engagement survey data. The person who has had this conversation with you knows that you see them as a full human being with a trajectory that matters, not just a role that needs to be filled.[55]

Beyond the annual Career Conversation, the day-to-day coaching work inside one-on-ones benefits from a simple framework. The GROW model, developed by Sir John Whitmore and widely used in executive coaching, provides a four-step structure for any development conversation: Goal, Reality, Options, Way forward.

Goal asks what the person is trying to achieve. Not the project goal, but their own development goal. What skill are they trying to build? What outcome are they trying to produce in this situation? Getting clarity on the goal before anything else prevents the conversation from jumping to solutions before the problem is understood.

Reality asks where things stand. What has the person already tried? What is getting in the way? What does the current situation look like honestly, without judgment? This step is about helping the person see their situation clearly, not about the manager diagnosing what is wrong.

---

55 Russ Laraway, When They Win, You Win: Being a Great Manager Is Simpler Than You Think (New York: St. Martin's Press, 2022).

Options asks for possible paths forward. This step should feel generative. What could they try? What have others done in similar situations? What would they do if the current approach did not constrain them? The manager's job here is to broaden the range of options the person is considering, not to select among them.

Way forward asks what the person will do. Specifically, by when, and how will they know whether it worked? This step converts a conversation into a commitment and gives the next one-on-one a concrete starting point.

The GROW model works because it keeps the problem-solving work in the hands of the person doing the developing. A manager who goes directly from "here is the problem" to "here is what you should do" has solved the immediate issue and built no capability. A manager who asks the four GROW questions has helped the person develop the judgment to solve the next version of this problem on their own.

Constructive Feedback

Constructive feedback is the most direct mechanism a leader has for developing people, and the one most data leaders are worst at. Mostly because they were never taught how to do it well and because the instinct to avoid uncomfortable conversations is nearly universal.

I struggled with this for my first few years as a leader. I was good at recognizing when things went right, but hesitated to give tough feedback. It wasn't until a mentor asked me a question that I changed how I thought about it entirely. "Do you actually care about the people on your team and want them to succeed?" I told her, of course I did. It's the most rewarding part of the job. It's why I like being a leader. "Then give the feedback," she said. "They'll know if you genuinely care about them, and that's how it will come across." She was right, and although conversations like that still aren't easy, I realized giving feedback is a part of caring for your team.

Give feedback as close to the event as possible. A comment delivered three weeks after a presentation has lost most of its impact. Give positive feedback in public when the context allows. Give corrective feedback in private. For significant issues, do not wait for the scheduled one-on-one if that is a week away.

The most reliable framework for delivering feedback is the Situation-Behavior-Impact (SBI) framework. Situation: the specific context ("in the architecture review meeting on Tuesday"). Behavior: what you observed, not an interpretation ("you interrupted the junior analyst twice before she finished her point"). Impact: the effect ("it undermined her confidence in front of the team and means I am less likely to get honest input from her in future meetings"). The SBI structure gives the person something specific enough to change, removing the interpretation layer that can make people defensive. "You were dismissive" is a character judgment. "You interrupted her twice" is an observation. The first invites argument. The second hopefully invites reflection.

After the SBI, stop talking. Resist the instinct to soften or immediately pivot to the positive. Let the feedback land. Then ask. What is your reaction to that?

The feedback sandwich, positive-corrective-positive, is so widely used that most people have learned to ignore the positives and wait for the "but." If you have something to recognize, recognize it. If you have something to correct, correct it. Mixing them dilutes both.

High performers need feedback too, specifically on the growth areas that will determine whether they develop into the senior contributors and eventual leaders the organization needs. The leaders who earn the deepest loyalty from their best people are almost always the ones who push them hardest, because those people know the difference between a leader who believes in their potential and one who avoids the discomfort of a development conversation. The best players want to be coached.

Performance Management

Performance management is, without question, one of the hardest parts of the job. The willingness to have these conversations anyway, with care, with specificity, and with genuine investment in the other person's outcome, is one of the clearest markers of a leader who takes their responsibility to their team seriously. Avoiding these conversations is not kindness. It is negligence, and the cost is paid by the individual who deserved honest feedback, by the team that has to absorb the gap, and by the organization's trust in the data leader's willingness to lead.

Kim Scott's Radical Candor framework describes the productive zone as the intersection of caring personally about the person and challenging them directly about the gap between their performance and what is needed. Ruinous empathy, caring personally but not challenging, feels kind in the short run and fails the person over time. Obnoxious aggression and challenging without caring produce defensiveness rather than growth. The combination of genuine care and direct challenge is the only kind of performance conversation that changes behavior.[56]

The most important distinction in performance management is between coachable behaviors and conduct issues, because the approach, timeline, and likely outcome are fundamentally different.

Coachable behaviors are skill gaps that can be addressed through feedback, development, and practice: an engineer who consistently underestimates work complexity, an analyst who produces technically sound work but cannot communicate it to

---

[56] Kim Scott, Radical Candor: Be a Kick-Ass Boss Without Losing Your Humanity (New York: St. Martin's Press, 2017).

non-technical audiences. The management approach is direct feedback, a specific improvement plan with measurable milestones, a defined timeline, and regular check-ins. Most coachable issues can be addressed in 60 to 90 days if the person is engaged.

Conduct issues differ in kind: a team member who is rude and hostile towards colleagues, or someone who misrepresents their work to leadership. These are not skill gaps. The management approach is a clear statement of what is not acceptable, documented examples, an unambiguous expectation that the behavior stops, and a defined consequence if it does not.

There is a cost to tolerating a known low performer beyond the low performer themselves, and it is one of the most reliable ways to lose your best people. High performers notice who consistently misses deadlines and faces no consequence. They notice who produces work the team quietly has to redo. They notice when they are the ones covering the gap, staying late to finish what someone else did not, taking the harder ticket because the easier one cannot be trusted to the teammate who has been struggling for six months with no visible action from their leader. Every day that gap goes unaddressed teaches your best people something specific: that the standard you talk about is not the standard you enforce, and that their own extra effort is quietly subsidizing someone else's comfort. High performers rarely quit over one bad performer. They quit, or disengage long before they quit, over the accumulated evidence that their leader will not act.

When continuous feedback is not producing the required change, a formal performance improvement plan (PIP) specifies the gap, the expected standard, the required improvements, the timeline, the support the organization will provide, and the consequence if improvement does not occur. Used honestly, a PIP is a development tool, not documentation before a predetermined termination.

Sometimes performance management ends in separation, and data leaders need to be prepared for that reality regardless of how it arrives. A team member may not improve despite a genuine PIP process. An organization may restructure in ways that eliminate a role. A hire may turn out to be wrong for the position despite a careful hiring process. Each situation is different in its cause and in how it is communicated, but the fundamentals of handling a separation with integrity remain the same.

Be prepared. Know exactly what the person is entitled to: severance, benefits continuation, references, outplacement support if the organization offers it. Have the paperwork ready before the conversation begins. A separation conversation that gets bogged down in uncertainty about what happens next adds unnecessary distress to an already difficult situation.

Be direct. The person deserves to know what is happening and why in plain language. Euphemisms create confusion about whether the decision is final and whether there is something to argue about. There is not. Say what is true.

The way you handle separations tells the remaining team everything about who you are and what the organization values. A separation handled with directness, preparation, and genuine care for the person leaving is one of the clearest signals a leader can send about the kind of organization they are building. A separation handled carelessly, or with obvious discomfort that prioritizes the leader's feelings over the departing employee's dignity, sends a different signal entirely, and the team will remember it.

Conflict Resolution

Conflict on a data team is a sign that people care about the work, not a sign that something has gone wrong. Engineers who have strong opinions about architectural decisions, analysts who disagree about methodology, data scientists who argue about model selection. This is exactly the intellectual energy that produces good work. The data leader's job is to keep it productive, not to eliminate it.

Organizational researchers distinguish between two types of conflict. Task conflict is disagreement about work: which approach is better, which use case to prioritize, whether the model's accuracy is sufficient for production deployment. Task conflict, managed well, improves decisions by surfacing perspectives that would otherwise be overlooked. Relationship conflict is personal: this person is difficult to work with, I do not trust their judgment, I feel dismissed in meetings. Relationship conflict is destructive. It degrades collaboration, drives away good people, and consumes the leader's time at a rate entirely disproportionate to what it produces.

The leader's job is to protect task conflict while preventing it from curdling into relationship conflict. That protection requires two active practices.

Address relationship conflict early. Relationship conflict left unaddressed compounds. What begins as one person feeling talked over in a meeting becomes a pattern of avoidance, culminating in two team members who will not collaborate directly. Intervening early, before the pattern is established, is far cheaper than intervening after it is. A direct, private conversation with each person separately, before bringing them together, is almost always the right first step. Ask each person what they are experiencing, not what the other person is doing wrong. The goal in the first conversation is understanding, not mediation.

Separate the people from the problem. Roger Fisher and William Ury's *Getting to Yes* (1981)[57] introduced the principle that most stuck conflicts are stuck because the parties are arguing over positions rather than interests. An engineer who insists the team must use platform A and an analyst who insists they must use platform B are in a position argument. An engineer who needs the

---

[57] Roger Fisher and William Ury, Getting to Yes: Negotiating Agreement Without Giving In (Boston: Houghton Mifflin, 1981).

platform to support real-time ingestion and an analyst who needs it to support complex ad hoc querying are in an interest conversation, and their interests may be compatible even when their positions are not. Helping both parties articulate what they need, rather than what they have decided they want, almost always reveals more room for agreement than either party expected.

A specific pattern to watch for in data teams is conflict between engineering and analytics about what counts as "good enough." Data engineers set quality standards and build tests that enforce them. Analysts need clean, reliable data to do their work. When those two functions are in tension, the conflict usually surfaces as frustration on both sides. Engineers feel their standards are being bypassed; analysts feel the engineering team is a bottleneck. This is a process problem masquerading as an interpersonal one. The solution is a documented, agreed-upon definition of what "production-ready" means for each data product, so the standard exists outside any individual relationship. When the standard is explicit, disagreements about whether something meets it are task conflict. When it is implicit and varies from person to person, it becomes relationship conflict.

The Culture Inside the Team

Everything this chapter has covered so far, including the candor, the vulnerability, the psychological safety, and the one-on-ones, adds up to something with a name. It is your team's culture, and you are building one whether you intend to or not. Forget the values poster and the team charter written at an offsite. Culture is the accumulated pattern of what happens. What gets celebrated, what gets ignored, what gets punished. Whether people admit mistakes early or bury them. Whether the loudest voice wins or the best evidence does. Whether "I don't know" is treated as honesty or weakness.

The most important thing to understand about culture is that what you tolerate sets it far more powerfully than anything you announce. You can declare that quality matters, but if you ship the rushed analysis anyway, the team learns the real standard. You can say you want bad news early, but if the messenger has a hard week after delivering it, the team learns to sit on problems. Every exception you make is a lesson, and the team studies you far more carefully than you study them.

Fostering a Data-Literate Culture

A persistent gap in data organizations is the assumption that the data team's job is to produce answers, and the business's job is to receive them. This model produces data organizations that are perpetually overwhelmed and businesses that are perpetually dependent.

Building data literacy means creating an organization where more people can read, interpret, and reason from data in their daily decisions, not at the same level as trained data scientists, but enough to formulate good questions, identify when something does not look right, and use data outputs to make better decisions without requiring an analyst to translate at every step. The Wavestone 2025 AI and Data Leadership Executive Benchmark Survey found that 92% of data leaders identify people and organizational change rather than technology as the primary barrier to a data-driven organization. This number has been stable for years. It is the finding the field has most systematically failed to act on.[58]

What works is anchoring literacy programs in specific business decisions and the data that informs them, segmenting participants by role and by how deeply each role needs to engage with data, building data-storytelling skills alongside technical fluency, and measuring behavioral outcomes rather than training-completion rates. Your role extends beyond running programs. It is the cumulative effect of every public example the data team sets, which includes the quality of its storytelling in leadership presentations, the accessibility of the dashboards it publishes, and the extent to which you visibly model data use in your own decisions and conversations.

---

[58] Wavestone, 2025 AI & Data Leadership Executive Benchmark Survey (Wavestone, 2025).

Retaining Talent

The cost of losing an employee in a data role ranges from 1.5 to 2.5 times base salary for mid-to-senior professionals, and 2 to 4 times for director-level and above, when you account for recruiting costs, lost productivity, ramp time for a replacement, and the institutional knowledge that walked out the door.

What employees consistently say they value are fair compensation, job security and stability, opportunities for growth and development (a powerful retention driver for data professionals specifically, given how fast the field changes), positive leadership and work environment, meaningful work, and flexibility. Robert Half's 2026 research found that 60% of job seekers prefer a hybrid work model combining home and office.[59] Among professionals who are not currently looking to leave, nearly half cite a desire to retain their flexibility as a key reason they stay. A rigid return-to-office mandate is a meaningful retention risk for data teams.

Career pathing is the long-term architecture of development. What does the path from junior analyst to senior analyst to analytics engineer to lead look like at your organization? What does the individual contributor track look like versus the management track? Employees who cannot see a path forward will eventually walk out the door to find one elsewhere. Make the path

---

59 Robert Half, 2026 workplace preferences research (Robert Half, 2026).

visible and remove the organizational obstacles that prevent people from following it. Your job is not to guarantee anyone a promotion. It is to make the criteria clear, the opportunities visible, and the developmental feedback honest enough that people can navigate toward what they want.

LinkedIn's 2025 Workforce Confidence Index found that employees who made one internal move had 41% lower attrition intent than those who did not, and those who made two or more internal moves had 59% lower attrition intent.[60] Internal movers understand the organization, data, business, and culture. They are productive faster. They are cheaper to develop than to replace. They bring something an external hire cannot: established relationships with the business partners who will champion the data team's work when it matters most.

Succession planning deserves specific attention given the realities of data leadership. A data function built entirely around the knowledge and relationships of a single leader is fragile. Identifying and developing successors, distributing institutional knowledge, and building a leadership bench within the data organization are among the highest-leverage investments you can make, both for the organization's continuity and for their own legacy.

Middle managers are the most underappreciated part of that bench. A data organization that grows beyond a handful of people

---

60 LinkedIn, 2025 Workforce Confidence Index (LinkedIn, 2025).

will eventually need team leads and senior practitioners who can carry day-to-day leadership without routing every decision through you. These are the people who run sprint ceremonies, conduct one-on-ones, manage stakeholder relationships at the working level, and make the hundreds of small judgment calls that keep the team functioning.

> *A data leader who has developed strong middle managers has built an organization that can absorb a leadership transition and scale into new business areas. A data leader who has not is the single point of failure at every level of the organization.*

Further Reading

Foundational works for going deeper on this topic:

Radical Candor, by Kim Scott, referenced earlier in this chapter; the fuller case for feedback that is both direct and personally invested.

When They Win, You Win, by Russ Laraway, the source of the career conversation framework this chapter draws on.

The Fearless Organization, by Amy C. Edmondson, the definitive treatment of psychological safety, and why it predicts team performance better than almost anything else.

Legacy Paper and Supply: Leading Data Talent

The data organization at Legacy is nine months old. The platform is running, the branch dashboard is live, the demand forecasting model is in development, and the team is small but functional. You are starting to discover something nobody warned you about when you took the job. Leading people is harder than building data products, and the skills that made you excellent at the technical work have almost nothing to do with the skills you now need.

Four situations in the past sixty days have made this clear.

The Coaching Moment

The data scientist comes to your desk on a Thursday afternoon with a problem. The demand forecasting model is producing predictions that look right for most product categories but under-forecasting demand for a specific set of high-margin paper products in the northeast branches. She has been looking at it for two days and cannot figure out why. She has the data open on her laptop. She is ready to walk through it together.

Your instinct is immediate and powerful. Sit down, look at the data, find the answer. You were a senior data scientist before you transitioned to leadership and you could probably find it faster than she can.

You do not sit down.

Instead, you ask: What have you already ruled out? She lists four hypotheses she has tested. You ask: What does the ordering pattern for those product categories look like compared to the ones the model is getting right? She pulls up a visualization. You ask: What is different about those products that might not be captured in the current feature set? She pauses. She pulls up the product master data. She finds it: those products have a longer lead time from the primary supplier, and the model has no feature for supplier lead time. Branches are placing larger buffer orders, which the model interprets as an organic demand signal rather than procurement behavior.

She found it. Not you. You asked four questions and got out of the way.

The insight she takes from this is technically useful. The insight she takes from being trusted to find it herself is more valuable and longer lasting. She is someone whose judgment can be relied upon, who does not need to be rescued, and whose development matters to her manager. That lesson does not come from being given the answer. It comes from being trusted to find it.

Take Blame. Give Credit.

Six weeks after the branch dashboard went live, the analytics engineer walks into your office and closes the door. There is a logic error in one of the gold-layer models she built. A filter condition that was supposed to exclude canceled orders has been excluding a different subset of orders due to a status code inconsistency in the source system, neither she nor the data engineer caught during testing. The dashboard has been showing understated sales figures for three weeks.

Your first response belongs to her, not to the error. She came forward the same day she found it. She traced it to the root cause. She has a fix ready to deploy. You tell her directly. Finding it, owning it, and fixing it is exactly what this team does. This is not a performance conversation.

Then you call the VP of Sales before the end of the day. Not to minimize the error or explain the technical nuance of status code inconsistencies. You say, "The branch dashboards have been showing incorrect sales figures for approximately three weeks due to an error in our data model. That is on me. The fix will be deployed tonight and we will send corrected figures to every branch manager by tomorrow morning."

Three months later, the demand forecasting model completes its first full quarter in production. The COO mentions it in the monthly leadership meeting and thanks you. Without hesitation, you say: "The data scientist did a great job building this model." She designed the feature engineering approach, she ran the validation, and she identified the supplier lead time variable that made the difference. This result belongs to her.

Take blame. Give credit. Every time, without exception. This is not generosity. It is the operating principle that determines whether the people on the team will take risks, surface problems early, and do their best work knowing you have their back.

It is worth making one clarification explicit. Taking blame and giving credit is not the same thing as protecting people from accountability. When the analytics engineer made an error, you did not tell the VP of Sales it was her fault. You told him it was yours, because it happened on your watch, in your organization, under standards you set and a review process you designed. That is where the accountability lived. Internally, the after-action conversation with her was direct and specific: what happened, why the testing process did not catch it, and what changes to the pipeline review workflow would prevent it in the future. She was not shielded from that conversation. She was not thrown under the bus in the leadership meeting.

Absorbing external blame while avoiding internal accountability conversations is not practicing this principle. That is conflict-avoiding. Holding the team to high standards privately and standing in front of them publicly is doing both jobs at once, maintaining the trust that makes people willing to surface problems, and maintaining the standards that make the organization worth trusting.

Coachable Behavior and Conduct

The data engineer is missing delivery commitments by an average of 30%. Business partners have noticed. You have been avoiding the conversation because she is technically excellent and hard to replace. That avoidance is ruinous empathy. The conversation happens: specific commitments, actual delivery dates, the gap. You agree on a practice. No commitment to a business partner goes forward without a review and an explicit buffer for unforeseen complexity. Three months later, the business relationship has recovered. That is a coachable behavior handled correctly.

Contrast that with the senior analyst who has been rude and hostile toward a junior team member. Talking over her in meetings, making sarcastic comments about her work in front of others, sending a message in the team Slack channel that two colleagues independently brought to you. When you address it directly, his response is to minimize it. That is a conduct issue, not a skill gap. The conversation is different in kind: you remind him what is not acceptable on this team, stated without ambiguity, with documented examples, and with a clear consequence if the behavior continues.

The next chapter covers stakeholder management, the practice of building and sustaining the organizational relationships that determine whether the data function can accomplish anything beyond what it can do on its own.

TWELVE

Stakeholder Management

There is a pattern in data leadership failures that repeats itself with consistency.

The data team builds something technically impressive. The infrastructure is sound, the governance is real, the models are performing, and the team is talented. And then, somewhere in the second or third year, the function stalls. Budget requests get deprioritized. Initiatives approved in January are quietly de-scoped by March. Business unit leaders stop attending the data council meetings. The CEO's enthusiasm, which was genuine at the beginning, is now directed at the AI vendor doing demos in the boardroom. And you look around, wondering what happened, because from where you stand, the work has been excellent.

What happened, almost always, is stakeholder management. Not a failure of technical execution. A failure of relationship, trust, and the organizational credibility that must be built continuously and deliberately with the people who decide whether the data function matters.

Tom Davenport and Randy Bean, who have tracked the CDO role for over a decade through the NewVantage Partners annual surveys, find that the most differentiating capability of long-tenured, high-impact data leaders is not technical excellence. It is the ability to translate data work into business value that executives care about, to build trust with people who do not share their technical fluency, and to navigate the organizational dynamics that determine whether good work gets funded and used.[61]

Stakeholder management is not a political game. It is the practice of understanding what the people your function depends on need, what they care about, what they are measured by, and what success looks like from their perspective, and then building a relationship in which your work visibly serves those things. A data leader who thinks about stakeholder management as impression management will optimize for appearing valuable. A data leader who thinks about it as genuine service will optimize for being valuable, which is more sustainable and ultimately more effective.

The structural reality is that data leaders typically have organizational scope wider than their formal authority. A CDO is accountable for how data is used across an entire organization but

---

[61] **Stakeholder Management:** Thomas H. Davenport and Randy Bean, NewVantage Partners (now Wavestone) annual Big Data and AI Executive surveys, published since 2012.

has direct authority only over the data team. Every other outcome the data leader is accountable for depends on the voluntary cooperation of people who do not report to them. Cooperation that is not grounded in genuine partnership will evaporate the first time it is inconvenient.

The Data Function as a Value Creation Center

The most important reframing you can make in every stakeholder relationship is about what kind of function the data organization is.

In most organizations, data and IT functions are budgeted, evaluated, and spoken about as cost centers. The business generates revenue; support functions enable the business to generate revenue. This framing sets the wrong terms for every conversation about investment, priority, and value.

> *When the data function is a cost center, the question about a budget request is "how much does this cost?" When the data function is a value creation center, the question is, "What does this generate?"*

The shift from cost-center to value-center positioning requires four things that are all leadership behaviors rather than technical ones. Connect every significant initiative to a business outcome someone other than the data team cares about: not "we are building a data lakehouse" but "we are building the infrastructure that will enable the marketing team to reduce their campaign analysis cycle from three weeks to two days." Quantify value in the language of the CFO: revenue impact, cost reduction, risk mitigation, and efficiency gains expressed in dollars are the currency of organizational investment decisions. Track what actually happened, not what was promised before the work began, because measuring and reporting on actual outcomes creates the credibility that future investment decisions rest on. And frame data failures in terms of business cost rather than technical problems; a data quality issue that caused incorrect inventory decisions cost the organization approximately $340,000 in excess carrying costs over the quarter it went undetected, which creates urgency to invest in prevention that "we had a data quality issue in the inventory tables" does not.

The Primary Stakeholder Relationships

Most new data leaders will not walk into a role where they are presenting to the CEO every month or negotiating territory with the Chief Information Officer (CIO). They will walk into a role where their most important relationships are with a VP of Sales who wants a dashboard that actually works, a finance manager who does not trust the numbers coming out of the data team's models, and an operations director who is skeptical that any of this will change how her team runs. Those are the relationships that determine whether the data function succeeds or fails, and they deserve as much strategic attention as any C-suite dynamic.

As data organizations mature and data leaders move into more senior roles, the stakeholder map expands upward. Eventually, you will need to manage relationships with a CFO who controls your budget, a CIO whose infrastructure you depend on, or a CEO whose sponsorship you need to survive a leadership change. Those relationships are addressed toward the end of this section. But for most readers of this book, the work starts closer to the ground.

Business Partners: Where Credibility Is Built

Business partners, the managers and directors who consume what the data team produces, are where the data function's credibility is established or destroyed one interaction at a time. The business partner relationship is primary.

The foundation of this relationship is starting with the business problem rather than the data solution. When the data team approaches a business partner with "we have built a new customer analytics capability, do you want to use it," the implicit message is that the team built something and now needs customers for it. When the approach is "we have been thinking about the churn problem you mentioned in the last team meeting, and we think there is a specific analysis that could help prioritize retention outreach," the implicit message is that the data team is paying attention to the partner's actual problems. The first approach asks the business partner to get excited about something the data team cares about. The second demonstrates that the data team has already been thinking about something the business partner cares about. That is a fundamentally different conversation.

Understanding what a business partner is measured on is a practical tool in stakeholder management. A sales manager measured on quota attainment sees data through a completely different lens than an operations manager measured on cycle time and defect rate. People are motivated by what they are accountable for, and the fastest path to a productive partnership is demonstrating that you understand what they are accountable for before you propose how data can help them.

A practical mechanism would involve a quarterly conversation between you and each major business partner, 30 to 45 minutes, covering what data initiatives are active, what outcomes have been produced, what is planned for the next quarter, and what the business partner's top priorities are that data could potentially support. These conversations do two things. They create a regular touchpoint that keeps the relationship from becoming transactional. And they produce the intelligence the data team needs to stay aligned with business priorities as they shift, which they always do.

Your Direct Leader and Managing Up

For a new data leader, the most important single stakeholder relationship is the one with whom they report to. This person controls budget allocation, organizational decisions, and the access that makes everything else possible. They are also the filter through which the data function's reputation reaches senior leadership. If your manager does not fully understand or believe in the value of the data function, you will find that budget conversations get deprioritized, hiring requisitions move slowly, and requests for executive visibility get quietly redirected.

The work here is the same as with any business partner, but the stakes are higher and the feedback loop is faster. Understand what your leader is trying to accomplish and show how the data organization contributes to it. Keep them informed about what the team is working on, what is going well, and which obstacles they can help clear. Do not let them be surprised by anything. A leader who is consistently informed, who always hears about problems from you before they hear about them from someone else, is a leader who advocates for you when it matters.

There is a discipline to building that relationship well, and it is underemphasized relative to how much it determines. Managing up means treating your relationship with your leader deliberately, just as you do the ones below and across you. The foundational reference is John Gabarro and John Kotter's Harvard Business Review article "Managing Your Boss," first published in 1980 and still reprinted decades later. Their central claim is uncomfortable and correct: managing the relationship with your leader is your responsibility, not theirs. Your leader is not omniscient and does not have unlimited bandwidth. If you assume that good work will be noticed, understood, and translated into budget and support on its own, you have made an assumption that will disappoint you.[62]

Two dynamics make this harder for data leaders than for most.

The first is domain knowledge. The person you report to will often not have deep expertise in the data space, and may have none in your specific corner of it. A CEO who rose through sales does not intuitively grasp why a governed semantic layer takes six months to build. A CFO who has spent a career in finance does not automatically see the difference between a dashboard and a production machine learning model, or why the latter requires infrastructure investment before it delivers results. This is not a failing on their part. It is a structural feature of the role: the work is technical enough that the people above you often have a limited picture of what it entails.

Closing that gap is your job, and you close it proactively. Explain what is hard and why. Explain why a request that sounds simple, "Can we just add that field to the dashboard?" sometimes requires three weeks of upstream work before it is possible. Do this not to

---

62 John J. Gabarro and John P. Kotter, "Managing Your Boss," Harvard Business Review, January 1980.

defend the team's pace but to give your leader the context to set better expectations with their own peers and to advocate for the resources you need. A leader who understands why the work is hard is a far better sponsor than one who is perpetually confused about why it takes so long.

The second is time horizon. Executives are frequently operating in quarters. Data and AI value tends to materialize over 12 to 36 months. You cannot make the value arrive faster than it does. What you can do is manage the gap with leading indicators. Measures that predict future value while the realized value is still accumulating. Adoption rates on new platforms, accuracy improvements in early model versions, reductions in manual work for business teams, and improvements in time-to-insight can all be reported long before the financial impact lands. Giving your leader those signals is how you keep support intact during the long middle of an initiative, when the work is real but the return has not yet shown up in a financial statement.

IT Partners

For data leaders who do not hold a C-level title, the IT relationship is less about organizational territory and more about practical collaboration. Data organization depends on IT infrastructure, including the network, cloud environment, access management systems, and change management processes. Treating IT as an obstacle to work around will have you spending significant energy fighting battles that do not need to be fought. By investing in the IT relationship early, you will find that access requests move faster, infrastructure decisions will account for the data team's needs, and that the inevitable moments of tension are lessened. Some will be resolved through conversation rather than escalation.

The most useful thing a new data leader can do with IT is to establish a shared understanding of who owns what. Data infrastructure and IT infrastructure overlap in ambiguous ways. Who manages the cloud environment the data platform runs in, who controls access to source systems, who owns the security review for new data tools. Clarifying those boundaries early, even informally, prevents the conflicts that arise when both teams assume the other is handling something and neither is.

Senior Leadership: When the Relationship Exists

For data leaders who do have regular access to a CFO, CIO, or CEO, a few principles are worth carrying into those relationships.

With a CFO, be specific about costs, conservative about benefit estimates, and clear about the measurement methodology that will evaluate whether the investment delivered. CFOs discount presentations that feel like advocacy rather than analysis. Presenting with the CFO's rigor standards rather than asking for exceptions to them earns a different kind of credibility. The CFO is also often a natural partner for financial analytics work. Things like planning, forecasting, and reporting automation. Building that partnership early, before the data function has its most sophisticated capabilities, creates a relationship of visible mutual value.

With a CIO, the data and IT organizations overlap in scope around data infrastructure, data security, system integration, and emerging technology. That overlap creates potential for conflict over ownership and decision rights. The practices that work include establishing a clear division of responsibilities early, identifying use cases where both functions depend on each other and resource them jointly, and maintaining a regular communication cadence that lets issues surface before they become conflicts. Territory disputes are best resolved by jointly drawing the map rather than fighting over individual parcels of land.

With a CEO or senior executive sponsor, communicate outcomes in business language, not technical updates. Early warning on risks before they become crises. A credible point of view on AI. Brief, disciplined communication that respects their time and gets to the point quickly. Showing up consistently prepared, concise, and focused on business outcomes builds the kind of executive trust that survives leadership changes and budget cycles.

Translating Technical Work for Non-Technical Audiences

The technical quality of the data team's work is invisible to most of the organization. What is visible is the communication around the work. This is the dimension of stakeholder management that most technically trained data leaders find most uncomfortable, because it requires simplification that can feel like misrepresentation. It is not. Communicating complex technical work clearly to a non-technical audience requires as much precision as the technical work itself.

Translate outputs into decisions. Every analysis should be presented in terms of what it enables someone to decide differently. "Here is what the data suggests about which customer acquisition channels produce your highest-lifetime-value customers, and what that implies for where to focus marketing spend in Q3" is a decision support tool. "Here is what the data shows about customer behavior" is a report.

Acknowledge uncertainty explicitly. Business leaders are not naïve; they know analysis involves judgment calls. Naming the assumptions, quantifying the uncertainty, and explaining what would need to be true for the analysis to be wrong will earn more trust than presenting point estimates as facts.

The So-What Discipline

The single most useful communication discipline you can develop is the so-what test. For every finding, every slide, every data point, ask "So what?" and keep asking until the answer is something a business leader cares about.

"Our data quality score improved from 76% to 84% this quarter." So what? "That means the customer churn model is running on more complete and accurate data." So what? "That means the retention predictions it generates are more reliable, and the sales team can trust the intervention recommendations more." So what? "That means we expect the team to convert a higher percentage of at-risk accounts, which should translate to roughly $1.8M in retained revenue annually if the conversion rate improvement materializes."

The final answer is something business leaders should be attentive to. The first answer is not. Most data reporting stops somewhere in the middle of that chain, where the audience understands that something improved without understanding why it matters to them. The so-what discipline pushes communication all the way to the answer the audience needed.

Executive Presence

The phrase has a mystique it does not deserve. Descriptions of executive presence tend toward charisma, a commanding voice, a certain suit. Strip away the consultant packaging and it comes down to how you behave in the room when the stakes are up, and every component of it can be practiced.

Composure is the first. When a CFO challenges your number in front of twelve people, the room is watching your reaction before it evaluates your answer. Defensiveness reads as doubt about your own work. The leader who says "good question, let me walk you through how we got there" and does it calmly has already won back the room, whatever the number turns out to be.

Answering the question that was asked is the second. You will lose executives by treating every question as an invitation to present. If the question was "is the migration on track," the answer is yes, no, or a date, followed by silence. Detail is available on request. Brevity signals command of the material.

The third is being honest at speed. "I don't know, and I will have you an answer by Friday," delivered without flinching, builds more credibility than a fluent guess. Executives spend their days being managed by people who are performing for them. The ones who stop performing stand out.

None of this requires you to change your personality. Quiet people have presence, and loud people can lack it entirely. Presence is the accumulated evidence that you stay steady under pressure, respect the room's time, and tell the truth when it would be easier not to. Every interaction either deposits into that account or draws it down.

Managing AI Expectations

Of all the expectations you manage, none right now demands more skill than managing expectations about AI. Every board has read that AI will transform the business. Every CEO has watched a competitor announce something. Every executive has used a consumer AI tool and concluded, reasonably, that the hard part is already solved. You are the person who stands in the gap between that expectation and what is true in your organization, and how you stand there determines whether the leadership team sees you as the one who will make AI real or the one standing in its way.

Start by respecting where the expectations come from, because dismissing them is its own kind of failure. The enthusiasm is not foolish. Executives see consumer tools that work in seconds, vendor demonstrations engineered to remove every rough edge, and a steady stream of headlines about agents that do everything. What they do not see is the data foundation, the governance, the integration, the evaluation, the reason your enterprise data does not behave like the clean example in the demo.

The expectation gap is, at bottom, a visibility gap.

The impressive part is loud and the hard part is silent, so leadership hears only half the picture.

Your job is not to puncture the enthusiasm. It is to give it somewhere real to go.

There are two ways to get this wrong, and both are common right now. The first is to become the obstacle, the leader whose answer to every AI request is "we cannot, our data is not ready." That answer may be true and it is still heard as the department of no, and it teaches executives to route around you. The second failure is more dangerous in this moment, because the pressure runs the other way. It is to say yes to everything, greenlight a flashy AI project with no foundation under it, and look current, right up until it fails in public and you own the failure. The pressure to appear AI-forward is enormous, and a leader who manages that pressure by overpromising is setting a trap for their own team. Managing expectations upward is, in part, protecting your people from commitments you cannot keep.

The move between those two failures is to meet enthusiasm with a credible point of view rather than a yes or a no. Tell them what is real and available now, what is a year out and what depends on it, and what is pure hype dressed as a roadmap. Then give the enthusiasm an outlet. An early, foundation-appropriate win that is realistically achievable. That gives leadership something real to say yes to, while you stay honest about the timeline for the ambitious thing. You are not refusing the vision. You are sequencing it, and sequencing is what turns "when will we have AI" into a plan the business can fund and follow.

Sometimes, though, the idea is not early. It is bad. A use case that does not fit the business, a tool someone wants because a competitor bought it, an agent aimed at a process that should not be automated at all. Saying no to a bad AI idea from a powerful person is the managing-up discipline under maximum pressure, and the mechanics are the same as saying no to any request. Do not deliver a flat refusal; make the cost and the risk visible, and hand the decision back. "We can build that. Here is what it would take, what happens if the data underneath it is wrong, and what I would recommend instead. Your call." The credibility you spend saying no to a bad idea is exactly what gives your yes any weight later.

This is the translator role at its hardest, standing between executive imagination and operational reality and refusing to lie in either direction. Get it right and you become the person the leadership team trusts to tell them the truth about AI, which is the most valuable position you can occupy right now. Get it wrong, as the obstacle or as the overpromiser, and you lose the room.

Navigating Difficult Stakeholder Relationships

Not every stakeholder relationship will be collaborative. Pretending otherwise is not useful.

For the skeptical business unit leader who has watched previous data initiatives overpromise and underdeliver, the strategy is not argument; it is demonstration. Identify the one problem this leader has that data can clearly and quickly help with, solve it well without asking for credit, and let the outcome do the persuasion. Skeptics converted by experience are much more durable allies than skeptics argued into position.

A final word on realistic expectations: no matter how skilled you become, there will almost certainly be stakeholders who remain difficult, skeptical, or actively resistant. Accept that reality without being defeated by it. Lean into the relationships that show genuine promise. Manage the ones that cannot be repaired without being consumed by them. Focus your energy on building the relationships that can be built, while managing the ones that cannot.

Practical Application: The Written Mandate and the First 90 Days

Most of what this chapter describes is built over years. But the foundation is laid in a specific window, and the window is short: your first 90 days.

Run the written mandate conversation in the first two weeks. Sit down with whoever you report to and document, explicitly, what the data function is accountable for, what decisions you have the authority to make, what resources have been committed, and what success looks like at six months, 12 months, and three years. If the organization has never been explicit about these things, the conversation will be uncomfortable, which is a good sign that it is necessary. The most consistently cited driver of short data-leader tenure, across the surveys and case studies in this space, is an ambiguous mandate. You build something, your leader expected something different, and the mismatch only surfaces after it has already turned political.

A short written mandate, specific and agreed to in writing, is the cheapest insurance you will ever buy against that failure.

In the first thirty days, do the listening tour. Meet with every major stakeholder individually, and do it to listen, not to present. What are their priorities? Which data problems are most painful for them right now? What was their experience with previous data initiatives? What would they need to see to believe this function deserves real investment? Asking questions rather than presenting answers produces intelligence you cannot get any other way, and it builds the kind of relationship that later meetings will depend on.

In the first sixty days, pick the early wins. Based on what the listening tour surfaces, choose one or two problems where the team can produce a visible, credible result quickly. Not the most technically interesting problems, but the ones that matter most to the stakeholders whose support matters most. Early wins do not have to be large. They have to be real, clearly attributable to the data team, and communicated in plain language.

In the first 90 days, start the cadence. Stand up the regular rhythms of stakeholder communication before you need them. The standing update with your leader, the quarterly reviews with business partners, the recurring one-on-ones. Establishing these while the stakes are low means they are already in place when a difficult conversation arrives and you need a channel that people trust.

Further Reading

Foundational works for going deeper on this topic:

The Trusted Advisor, by David Maister, Charles H. Green, and Robert M. Galford, the classic framework for building the kind of credibility you have to earn before you can spend.

Never Split the Difference, by Chris Voss, a former FBI negotiator's take on influence and difficult conversations, more directly useful for managing up than it sounds.

Influence Without Authority by Allan R. Cohen and David L. Bradford, the foundational text on getting things done through people who don't report to you.

Legacy Paper and Supply: Stakeholder Management

The New COO

Eight months into TDS execution, Legacy hires a new Chief Operating Officer. He comes from a distribution company twice Legacy's size with a reputation for operational efficiency and cost discipline. He is skeptical of what he finds: a data organization with nine people, a $1.5 million budget, and a three-to-five year roadmap full of initiatives that have not yet delivered most of their projected value. In his first week, he asks the CFO a pointed question: "What are we getting for this investment?"

You find out about the question secondhand. This is not a surprise. It is the situation every data leader faces when a leadership change brings in someone who did not sponsor the data strategy and does not feel ownership of its outcomes.

The wrong response is to send the new COO a deck summarizing the TDS roadmap and projected ROI. The right response starts with a meeting request, not a deliverable. You ask for 45 minutes in his first two weeks. Not to present. You ask: What are the two or three operational problems keeping you up at night, and is there anything the data organization should be doing differently to be more useful to you?

That question does two things. It signals you are not defensive about the scrutiny. And it inverts the dynamic from "let me explain why we deserve our budget" to "tell me what you need."

The COO, who expected to be lobbied, is instead asked a genuine question. The conversation lasts 90 minutes.

You learn he has deep concerns about inventory management, specifically the cost of expedited shipping when stockouts occur. He did not know Legacy's team was already building a forecasting model. He also wants to see branch-level operational performance data the way the VP of Sales sees sales performance data.

The TDS roadmap has two use cases that directly address his concerns. You do not announce this triumphantly. You describe what is being built, what it will produce, and when. You ask whether those deliverables would be useful to him. He says yes with some alterations. You ask whether any team initiatives should be deprioritized in favor of his priorities. That question earns more trust than any amount of ROI projection.

Within 90 days, the COO is the one who mentions the forecasting model's performance improvement in a leadership team meeting where you are not present.

He is not a data evangelist. He does not need to be. He is a senior leader who now sees the data organization as solving problems he cares about, which is the only form of organizational support that holds when budgets get tight or priorities shift.

If you had treated the new COO as a threat to be managed, you would have spent those 90 days building a defensive presentation. Instead, you treated him as a stakeholder to be partnered with and spent that time building an ally. The difference between those two approaches is not strategic sophistication. It is the willingness to lead from curiosity rather than from fear.

One Conversation at a Time

The CEO has asked for a monthly leadership team presentation on the data organization's progress, starting next month. The new COO, who arrived skeptical and has only recently begun to engage, will be in the room.

The first move is not to build slides. It is to have individual conversations with each member of the leadership team in the two weeks before the first presentation. The CEO, CFO, COO, and VP of Sales each get a thirty-minute conversation with the same opening question. What would make this monthly update useful to you?

The CEO wants to know that the AI initiatives the board keeps asking about are being approached thoughtfully and that Legacy will roll them out as soon as possible. The CFO wants to know whether the data investments are paying off in any measurable way. The COO wants to know whether the forecasting work will make a dent in the inventory carrying costs he identified as a priority in his first week. The VP of Sales wants to know whether the branch dashboard is changing how branch managers run their teams, or whether it is another tool that got launched and quietly stopped being used.

None of these are the same question. None of them are answered by a slide that says "here is what we built this quarter."

The first monthly presentation is built entirely around those four specific answers. Eight slides. The first lists the three active initiatives and the business problem each solves, in one sentence each. The next four give one update each, written in the vocabulary of the leader it is for, with quantified outcomes where they exist and honest uncertainty where they do not. The sixth names one risk or issue that needs leadership attention and what is being asked of the leadership team. The seventh lists the two things the data organization needs from the room to move forward. The eighth shows what is planned for the next 90 days.

The presentation runs 20 minutes. The discussion runs 40. The COO asks three pointed questions about the forecasting model's timeline and the assumptions behind the carrying cost estimate. You answer two of them directly and say "I don't have a confident answer on that one yet" on the third. The COO writes something down.

The VP of Sales pulls you aside: "I'm glad to hear you understood the sales problem the way you do. I worried you were just building models." That comment contains the entire thesis of this chapter. Being seen as someone who understands the business's problems will always generate more organizational support than being seen as someone who just builds models. The models are how the problem gets solved. Understanding the problem is what earns the right to solve it.

Branch Skeptic

Not every stakeholder relationship operates at the C-suite level. One of Legacy's branch managers has been vocal about his skepticism of the dashboard, telling his team that the numbers do not match what he knows from the field. He is not being obstructionist. He has watched systems come and go at Legacy for fifteen years. His resistance is a stakeholder management problem, not a technical one.

You visit his branch in person and spend two hours asking him to walk through exactly where the dashboard numbers diverge from his intuition about the business. Not to defend the dashboard. Not to explain the data model. To understand the gap.

You find three discrepancies. Two turn out to be data quality issues in the branch's order entry process you were not aware of: product category codes entered inconsistently by the order desk for years, producing category-level analytics that do not match what the branch manager knows about his product mix. One turns out to be a definition difference: the dashboard uses the agreed-upon governance definition of an active account, while the branch manager has been using a broader definition that includes accounts that have placed any order in the past 18 months. Neither of them is wrong. They are using different definitions, and the governance work that resolved this at the organizational level has not been fully communicated at the branch level. That is your gap to close, not his.

By the end of the visit, the branch manager is not a convert. But he has agreed to pilot the dashboard with three of his sales representatives for the next 60 days and to share specific feedback on what works and what falls short. You leave him a notebook with his name on the cover and a note, "Your feedback in the next sixty days will make this better for every branch. Thank you for being honest about what can be improved."

That gesture is not theatrical. It is a signal: your experience with this tool matters, you are a partner in making it better, and we are not going to declare victory and disappear.

Stakeholder management is not a project with a completion date. It is the ongoing condition of data leadership, and the leaders who do it well are not those who have mastered it but those who keep practicing it. Conversation by conversation, relationship by relationship, month by month.

The next chapter covers effective change management. The discipline that determines whether the organizational transformations the data function seeks to produce take hold.

THIRTEEN

Effective Change Management

Data leaders live at the intersection of two distinct change realities.

The first is internal. The data organization itself is in near-constant change: new tools emerge and old ones are deprecated, cloud platforms evolve faster than teams can fully adopt them, governance programs are built and rebuilt as organizational needs grow, and machine learning models are retrained, replaced, or retired. The data professional who is not comfortable with continuous change is in the wrong field.

A business partner once asked me, half-joking, when the data organization was going to stop "modernizing." We finish one initiative and start the next, he said, and it never seems to end. I told him it would stop the day the business stopped wanting to do new things and technology stopped changing. We both laughed, but he was not wrong to notice the pattern, and I was not wrong about why it exists. There is no finish line here, only a direction of travel, and if you are waiting for the moment when everything finally settles down, you will be waiting for the rest of your career.

The second change reality is external. The data organization is also, by its very nature, a change agent for the rest of the business. An analysis is requested because a business leader is considering a change. A dashboard is built because the business wants to change how it monitors performance. A governance program is implemented because the organization needs to change how it manages and trusts its data. A machine learning model is deployed because the business wants to change how it makes decisions that were previously made by intuition. In almost every case, the data team's output is an input to someone else's change process.

McKinsey has tracked digital transformation outcomes for years. Only about 16% succeed in sustainably improving performance. The rest either fall short of their objectives, produce short-term gains that erode over time, or fail outright. This is not because organizations hire bad technologists or build bad platforms. It is because technology without behavior change is just technology, and behavior change is what most transformation programs systematically underinvest in.[63] Prosci, which has run the largest ongoing benchmarking study in change management across more than 10,000 practitioners since 1998, puts the upside case in equally stark terms: organizations that apply excellent change

---

63 **Effective Change Management:** McKinsey & Company, global survey research finding that only 16 percent of respondents report their organizations' digital transformations successfully improved performance.

management are roughly seven times more likely to meet or exceed their objectives than those that apply poor change management.[64] The technology is equivalent. The change management is what separates the outcomes.

Technical Problems and Adaptive Challenges

Before any framework makes sense, there is a conceptual distinction that will reframe everything else in this chapter. Ronald Heifetz and Marty Linsky draw a line between two fundamentally different kinds of problems.

A **technical problem** is one where the challenge is well-defined, expertise exists, and someone with the right knowledge can deliver the solution. Migrating a data warehouse to a cloud platform is a technical problem. It is difficult, it requires skilled engineers, and it will take longer than anyone originally predicted. But the path forward is known and success is measurable.

An **adaptive challenge** is different. Adaptive challenges are those in which no existing expertise fully solves the problem and in which progress requires people to change their beliefs, habits, loyalties, or values. Getting a leadership team that has made decisions on gut instinct for thirty years to change how they use

---

64 Prosci, Best Practices in Change Management benchmarking report, based on over 10,000 practitioner responses collected since 1998.

data is an adaptive challenge. Getting a business unit to accept that the data team's definition of "active customer" supersedes the one they have been using for a decade is an adaptive challenge. Getting an organization to trust AI recommendations enough to act on them is an adaptive challenge.

The most common and most expensive failure mode in data transformation is treating adaptive challenges as technical problems. The logic goes: the organization does not use data to make decisions; therefore, we need better dashboards; therefore, we will build better dashboards; and then the organization will use data. The dashboards get built. They sit largely unused. You conclude the business is resistant. The business concludes the data team does not understand what the organization needs. Both conclusions are wrong. What happened is that you solved a technical problem nobody had while leaving the adaptive challenge completely untouched.

Before committing resources to a data initiative, ask whether success depends primarily on getting a technology to work, or primarily on getting people to behave differently. If the honest answer is the second, you are looking at an adaptive challenge, and the change management work is the main event.

What People Experience During Change

Organizational change programs are designed at the level of the organization. None of that directly addresses what is happening in the mind of an individual human being who is being asked to change how they work.

William Bridges made the essential contribution here in *Managing Transitions* (1991). Change and transition are not the same thing. **Change** is situational and external: the new platform goes live, the governance policy is published. **Transition** is psychological and internal: the process a person goes through to relinquish their old way of working and build a new identity around the new way.[65]

Bridges' model has three phases. The **Ending** is what people must let go of before the change can take root. This is the phase most change programs skip, because it is uncomfortable to acknowledge that asking people to adopt something new also means asking them to give something up. The analyst who built the Excel model the whole team depends on is being asked to let go of the expertise, the social value, and the sense of indispensability that model gave them. That is a real loss, and it deserves acknowledgment.

---

65 William Bridges, Managing Transitions: Making the Most of Change (Reading, MA: Addison-Wesley, 1991).

The **Neutral Zone** is the disoriented, anxious period between letting go of the old way and fully inhabiting the new one. People in the Neutral Zone know the old way no longer applies but have not yet developed competence or confidence in the new way. Performance typically drops during this period, which is an important thing to communicate to executives before launching a transformation.

The productivity dip is not evidence that the change is failing. It is evidence that the transition is happening.

The **New Beginning** is when people have developed genuine competence in the new way and begin to experience it as normal rather than imposed. New Beginnings cannot be forced or scheduled. They emerge when people have had enough time, support, and successful experience with the new approach to internalize it.

ADKAR: Understanding Change at the Individual Level

Alongside organizational steps, there is a parallel frame for what must happen in every individual affected by the change. The ADKAR model, developed by Jeff Hiatt and Prosci, identifies five building blocks each person must develop for a change to succeed.

Awareness of the need for change. Before a person can move toward a new way of working, they must understand why the old way is no longer sufficient. An analyst who is told "we are implementing data governance" has received information. An analyst who understands "the inconsistent definitions across our dashboards caused the executive team to make inventory decisions based on conflicting numbers, costing us $3M last year" has reached Awareness.

Desire to support and participate. Awareness creates the rational case. Desire is the motivational piece. "This is good for the company" is not usually enough of a reason to change behavior. Desire cannot be mandated. It can be cultivated through honest communication, through addressing real concerns, and through demonstrating that the change is being led by people who have thought about what it means for the people going through it.

Knowledge of how to change. Even people who are aware of the need and desire the outcome cannot change without knowing what specifically they are supposed to do differently. Most change programs are clear about the what and the why, and completely vague about the how.

Ability to implement the required behaviors. Knowledge is theoretical. Ability is demonstrated. Training completion is not ability. Demonstrated performance in the new way of working is ability.

Reinforcement that sustains the change. The behaviors that get reinforced are the behaviors that persist. Without reinforcement, people revert, not because they are lazy, but because reverting is what all humans do when the new behavior has not been anchored by enough successful repetition and positive consequence.

The diagnostic value of ADKAR is significant. When a change is struggling, most leaders respond with more communication, which addresses Awareness. But if the population has already reached Awareness and the gap is at Desire, more communication makes the problem worse by signaling that leadership does not understand the actual obstacle.

The Change Management Process

The steps below draw on Kotter's foundational work, Prosci's benchmarking research, and the McKinsey Influence Model.[66] In practice, they are overlapping and iterative workstreams, not a linear march.

Understand the current state. Every effective change program begins with an honest assessment of where the organization is, not where leadership wishes it were. The history with previous initiatives matters as much as the current technical state. An

66 John P. Kotter, Leading Change (1996); Prosci benchmarking research; McKinsey & Company, "The Influence Model: Ten Guiding Principles of Change Management," McKinsey Quarterly, 2003.

organization that tried data governance two years ago and abandoned it is not the same context as one launching governance for the first time. The residue of past failures shapes how the organization will hear the new initiative, and stakeholders who have been burned before are not being irrational when they are skeptical.

Create urgency. Kotter identifies this as the most underinvested step in failed change programs. The distinction that matters is between declared urgency, a leadership announcement, and created urgency, when people at all levels can see and feel the gap between where the organization is and where it needs to be. For data initiatives, threat framing tends to be more reliable; "our data quality issues cost us $3M last year" is harder to rationalize away than "better data could make us more competitive."

Create a vision. A compelling vision gives urgency somewhere to go. Without it, urgency produces anxiety. The vision should be co-created rather than handed down; when the people who will live inside the changed state have had genuine input into what that state looks like, their ownership of it is real. When a vision is developed by the data team and announced to the business, the business receives it as something being imposed on them.

Build the coalition. Effective change requires two distinct groups. Champions are credible peer-level influencers distributed across functions whose adoption of a new practice signals to their colleagues that it is worth adopting. They are identified because their peers already trust them. Allies are the formal authority holders whose active sponsorship gives the initiative organizational weight. Prosci has named active and visible executive sponsorship as the number one contributor to change success in every study it has run since 1998.[67] Not nominal sponsorship, a name on a kick-off email. Active sponsorship means the executive is regularly and publicly using the new tool and making it visible that this initiative has their genuine attention.

Communicate the change. Communication runs as a parallel workstream, not a phase, from the first awareness-building conversation through the final anchoring of new behaviors. Two Prosci findings matter: employees want to hear the organizational rationale from senior leaders, and they want to know what the change means for their day-to-day work from their direct manager. A CEO email does not tell an analyst what they are supposed to do differently on Monday morning. That translation is the manager's job. And a message needs five to seven exposures across different channels before it transitions from information to conviction.[68]

Implement and remove barriers. Pilot before full rollout. Phase the rollout deliberately. Remove barriers actively. In data organizations, barriers are typically one of four things: technical

---

67 Prosci, Best Practices in Change Management, 12th ed., based on 25 years of research from 10,800+ professionals globally.

68 Prosci, Best Practices in Change Management, 12th ed., which covers communication frequency and message reinforcement as part of its core benchmarking findings.

blockers, process conflicts, skill gaps, or cultural resistance, each requiring a different intervention.

Monitor and sustain. Measurement requires three layers: activity metrics (Are we doing what we said we would do?), adoption metrics (Are people changing their behavior?), and outcome metrics (Is the business better?). Kotter identifies premature declaration of victory as a reliable predictor of transformation failure. When leadership announces that the change has been achieved, the systems holding it in place simultaneously relax, and the change, not yet fully anchored in culture, begins to unravel.

Manage resistance.

Resistance is not the enemy of change. It is information about the change, delivered by the people closest to the impact.

The most powerful resistance-management practice is proactive identification before resistance becomes organized. By the time resistance is organized, the cost of addressing it has already increased significantly.

Further Reading

Foundational works for going deeper on this topic:

Managing Transitions, by William Bridges, referenced earlier in this chapter; the fuller model of the psychological transition underneath any organizational change.

Leading Change, by John P. Kotter, the eight-step model this chapter's change process is built on.

ADKAR: A Model for Change in Business, Government, and Our Community, by Jeff Hiatt, the individual-level complement to Kotter's organizational model, and the source of the ADKAR framework used in this chapter.

Legacy Paper and Supply: Effective Change Management

The branch manager who agreed to pilot the dashboard with three of his sales representatives gave you an honest assessment at the end of month one. Two of the three were using it daily and finding it useful; one was not using it at all and had made clear she did not intend to.

Three months later, the results are instructive.

The two enthusiasts have become genuine champions. They use the dashboard daily, flagging account activity alerts, and, in two cases, have had proactive conversations with customers about declining order frequency before those accounts reduced their spend. One of those conversations produced a retained account worth approximately $180,000 annually.

The third salesperson is still not using the dashboard. She has been with the company for nineteen years and has built a mental model of her territory through thousands of customer interactions. She says the data is wrong. When pressed, she says it does not capture the relationship context she relies on. A customer flagged as showing declining order patterns is not at risk because she talked to them last week and they are fine, and a model cannot know what she knows from nineteen years in that territory.

You have two choices. Treat this as a resistance problem and design a communication intervention about data accuracy. Or treat it as information and investigate whether she is right.

You dig in and it turns out she is partly right. The demand pattern model flags accounts based on trends in order frequency and volume. It has no visibility into the qualitative relationship signals that experienced salespeople pick up from direct conversation. In two of the cases she disputes, she is wrong. The model is capturing a genuine decline in order frequency that she has rationalized away. In one case, she is right. The account is in a planned temporary reduction that she knows, from direct knowledge, will reverse next quarter. The model is calling it at-risk when it is not.

What actually needs addressing is not her resistance so much as what the model can and cannot see, and whether the data team was sufficiently honest with the sales team about those limitations when the dashboard launched.

Using the ADKAR lens, her situation is clear. She has Awareness and Knowledge. What she lacks is Desire, and Desire cannot be created through more communication about data accuracy. It can only be created by demonstrating that the tool is useful to her in the way she works, and by showing that the people building it care about what she knows.

The intervention is a working session, not a communication campaign. You go to the branch in person and run a session with the full sales team. In cases where the model flagged an account you believed was fine, what did you know that the model did not? The output is a set of qualitative signals that experienced salespeople use to assess account health, not currently in the feature set: recent conversations with the account, known temporary situations affecting the customer's business, and relationship factors that explain anomalous order patterns. The data team begins working with sales operations to explore how qualitative account notes could be incorporated into the model's feature engineering.

The resistant salesperson does not become a champion overnight. But she agrees to flag accounts where she believes the model is wrong, with a brief explanation of what she knows that the model does not. The data team tracks whether her override judgment outperforms the model on those specific accounts. It often does. Three months later, this becomes the foundation for a human-in-the-loop feedback mechanism that materially improves the model's performance on the edge cases where experienced relationship knowledge matters most.

What happened here maps directly onto Bridges' transition model. The resistant salesperson was in the Ending phase. She was being asked to let go of something real: nineteen years of expertise and the professional identity that came with being the person whose judgment could not be replicated by a system. Her knowledge was acknowledged as valuable, not as an obstacle to be overcome. The human-in-the-loop mechanism moved her into the New Beginning by giving her a meaningful role in making the model better, not by persuading her it was already right.

The governance rollout scheduled for the following quarter is now being designed with all of this in mind.

The first question is urgency. You have a real urgency catalyst. The CFO recently discovered that Legacy's finance and sales teams are reporting different active customer counts, differing by over 20%, because each team has been using its own definition for years. That discrepancy is not an abstract governance problem. Executive decisions about customer retention investment, sales territory planning, and revenue forecasting are being made on numbers that do not agree with each other. The framing for the governance rollout will not be "we are implementing governance." It will be "we are solving the problem where our customer data gives us two different answers to the same question, and that inconsistency is costing us in decisions we cannot fully trust."

The second question is coalition. You identify three people to anchor the guiding coalition. The branch manager himself. He has moved from skeptic to engaged participant, and his willingness to engage with the data team carries credibility across the branch network that a central team member cannot replicate. A senior finance analyst who has been frustrated by the active account discrepancy for two years. She already has desire. She needs knowledge and a vehicle for her energy. The sales operations lead who helped build the human-in-the-loop feedback mechanism. She has seen the data team listen and respond, and she is willing to vouch for that experience to her peers in other functions.

None of these three people are being appointed to a governance committee. They are being asked to co-design the solution to a problem they have already told you they care about. Governance committees generate compliance at best. Co-designers generate ownership.

The governance work that began in Part 1 established the definition. The change management work that begins here is what makes that definition stick.

The next chapter covers scaling data organizations, how to grow the function, manage increasing complexity, and build the institutional structures that allow a data organization to compound its value over time.

FOURTEEN

Scaling Data Organizations

Something starts to feel wrong before you can name what it is. The team is working harder than it ever has and producing more. The backlog is longer than ever. The requests are more sophisticated than they were a year ago. The infrastructure that was perfectly adequate when the team was four people is starting to creak under the demands of a team that is now twenty. The governance process that two people could manage with a shared spreadsheet is producing bottlenecks now that sixteen people need to coordinate around it.

This is what scaling feels like in practice. Not a single dramatic inflection point. A gradual accumulation of signals that the organization being run today is not the organization that tomorrow's ambitions require.

Most of the writing on scaling data organizations was produced by engineers and leaders at large technology companies whose data teams had hundreds of people and an engineering culture that treats data infrastructure as a core product. That is not most data leaders' reality. Most are running teams of five to thirty people inside organizations where data is important but not the primary business. This chapter is written for that reality.

Understanding Where You Are

Before making good scaling decisions, you need an honest assessment of where the organization currently sits on the maturity curve. The instinct is to assume you are further along than you are. Research from Gartner finds that most organizations cluster at the lower and middle levels of data maturity, and fewer than 10% reach the highest levels of transformational capability. The executives who believe their organization is further ahead than it actually is invest in capabilities their foundation cannot yet support.

Several credible frameworks exist. Gartner's five-level model runs from Basic through Opportunistic, Systematic, Differentiating, and Transformational. Most organizations sit at levels two and three. The CMMI Data Management Maturity model scores data management practices across five levels and is widely used in regulated industries. The EDM Council's DCAM is the standard in financial services.

What all of these frameworks agree on is that maturity does not happen quickly. Moving through one meaningful level in a large enterprise typically takes three to five years. The data leader who sets a 12-month expectation for becoming a "data-driven organization" is setting up for a credibility problem. The data leader who sets a realistic three-year roadmap with visible milestones at six and 12 months is setting up for a conversation the business can participate in.

The barriers to advancing maturity are almost never primarily technical. Gartner, MIT, and the Wavestone benchmark surveys all find that cultural challenges, organizational dynamics, and talent gaps are the dominant impediments. The organization that buys a more sophisticated platform without addressing its cultural and governance maturity will end up with a more expensive version of the same problems it already had.

Building With Growth in Mind

The single most expensive mistake in data organization design is building for today's scale and being surprised when tomorrow's scale breaks it. This does not mean over-engineering for scale you will not reach for years. It means making architectural, process, and organizational decisions with explicit awareness of what will need to change at the next level of scale.

Three principles for small to mid-sized data organizations:

- **Build for observability from the start**: Data pipelines that fail silently, quality issues that surface only when a business user complains, model drift that nobody detects until the predictions stop making sense. All of these are scaling problems that originated in the absence of observability. The investment feels like overhead when the team is small and everyone knows what everything does. It becomes essential when the team doubles in size.
- **Document aggressively and early**: The knowledge that lives only in one person's head is a scaling liability. When that person leaves, the knowledge leaves with them. Documentation is the mechanism by which a small team's knowledge becomes an organizational asset that survives team changes.
- **Design processes to scale**: A process that works because two people both know what to do is not the same as one that works because it is clearly defined and can be followed by someone new. Building the process infrastructure that scales with the team is leadership work, not administrative work.

Understanding Business and IT Roadmaps

Scaling decisions made in isolation from the broader organizational context produce data organizations that are impressively capable in ways that do not match what the business needs. Building toward self-service analytics while the business is planning a major ERP migration is building in the wrong direction.

Understanding the business roadmap means knowing which strategic initiatives are planned over the next one to three years and what data capabilities they will require. Understanding the IT roadmap means knowing which infrastructure changes are planned and ensuring the data function's technical decisions align with them. The key conversations to have are which platforms IT is planning to consolidate, which system migrations are planned that will change source data, and where the agreed boundary is between IT and data responsibilities.

The Messy Middle

There is a phenomenon that data leaders at growing organizations encounter with enough regularity that it deserves a name. Call it the messy middle.

The messy middle happens when the data organization has grown large enough that informal coordination no longer works, but has not yet built the formal structures that replace it. Things fall through the cracks that never used to. The documentation that two people maintained in their heads is no longer shared knowledge for a team of ten. The ad hoc prioritization that worked when you had visibility into every active request is breaking down under volume. You are spending more time on coordination and conflict resolution and less time on strategy and stakeholder relationships.

The messy middle is not a failure. It is a predictable inflection point that every growing data organization passes through. The failure is not recognizing it and responding deliberately.

The response is to build the formal structures that informal coordination previously handled. Documented processes that new team members can follow, defined decision rights that do not require your involvement in every judgment call, team structure with clear ownership, and communication rituals that maintain coordination at the team level.

The messy middle is also the moment when your job changes most significantly. The leader who is still trying to stay close to every technical decision is becoming the bottleneck. The transition to leading through others, delegating technical decisions with clear intent and criteria, and focusing personal attention on strategy, stakeholders, and team development, is the leadership version of the scaling challenge.

Assessing Infrastructure for Scale

A scaling infrastructure assessment asks what will break first under increased load, what is already accumulating technical debt, and what architectural decisions made at smaller scale are now constraints on growth.

- **Pipeline health and observability**: Are pipelines reliable, monitored, and well-documented? Pipelines that worked when one engineer understood the whole system become organizational liabilities when that engineer is gone.
- **Platform architecture and flexibility**: Can the current platform handle higher data volumes, more users, and more complex queries without a major redesign? The lakehouse architecture, combining the flexibility of a data lake with the performance of a data warehouse, has become the dominant pattern for scalable data infrastructure in 2026.
- **Data quality and governance infrastructure**: Is quality monitored systematically or discovered reactively through business complaints? The governance infrastructure that is adequate when one team uses the data will not be adequate when five teams use it.
- **Tool inventory**: Data organizations accumulate tools faster than they rationalize them. Tool sprawl is a real and expensive problem. The scaling assessment should identify which tools are earning their cost, which are duplicating capabilities, and which represent debt that needs to be resolved.

Managing Technical Debt

Technical debt is the accumulated cost of shortcuts, compromises, and deferred work that builds up over the life of a data system. Every time a data engineer hardcodes a transformation instead of building a reusable process, builds a pipeline without documentation or monitoring, or skips data quality tests because the deadline is tomorrow, they are taking out a loan against the system's future maintainability. The problem is when the debt is never repaid.

Technical debt is commonly estimated to consume a substantial share of IT budgets, and a significant portion of engineering time goes toward managing it rather than building new capabilities. There is a specific risk as AI adoption accelerates. Layering AI capabilities on top of unmanaged technical debt produces compounding fragility. An AI model trained on data from poorly governed pipelines will produce unreliable outputs. The technical debt in the data foundation is a risk management problem for every AI system built on top of it.

Three practices manage data technical debt deliberately. Make the debt visible through an inventory of known items rated by severity and by the cost of not addressing them. Budget for remediation explicitly. Mature data organizations typically dedicate 15% to 25% of engineering capacity to debt reduction rather than new capability development. Build debt prevention into the definition of done. New pipeline work that does not include documentation, monitoring, and tests is not finished.

Cloud Cost Management

Cloud computing has made data infrastructure radically more accessible and radically more variable in cost. The FinOps Foundation reported in their 2026 State of FinOps survey that virtually all organizations, 98%, are now managing AI spend through FinOps practices, up from 31% in 2024.[69] Running cloud and AI infrastructure without financial governance routinely leads to cost surprises that undermine budget credibility.

Core FinOps practices:

- Tag workloads by team, project, and use case so costs can be attributed to specific data products.
- Show teams what their workloads cost before creating formal chargeback mechanisms.
- Build cost estimates into the development process so engineers understand cost implications before they ship.
- Automate anomaly detection on cloud spend with alerts when costs deviate from baseline. Organizations with

---

[69] **Scaling Data Organizations:** FinOps Foundation, 2026 State of FinOps Survey (FinOps Foundation, 2026).

mature FinOps practices consistently report substantial cost reductions on cloud infrastructure spend.

Scaling AI and Machine Learning

The bottleneck is almost never the algorithms. It is the operational infrastructure for managing models throughout their lifecycle, MLOps.

At the earliest stage, models are trained and deployed manually, with no systematic monitoring, automated retraining, or version control. This works for one or two models. It does not scale to five or ten. At the intermediate stage, the organization has model version control, basic performance monitoring, and a defined retraining process. Models are tracked in a model registry, and retraining is triggered manually when performance degrades. This is where most small to mid-sized data organizations should aim before scaling AI capabilities further. At the advanced stage, model training, validation, and deployment are automated in a continuous pipeline and feature engineering is managed through a feature store.

Invest in the operational infrastructure for your current model count before building more models.

A portfolio of ten poorly managed models produces less value and more risk than a portfolio of three well-managed ones.

Hiring for Scale: Bottlenecks First

The key hiring principle at scale. Start with the capabilities required by current use cases, not the org chart you eventually want. At any given stage, one or two capability gaps are constraining everything else. Hiring to relieve those specific bottlenecks produces compounding returns. Hiring to fill roles that are not yet bottlenecks creates expensive, underutilized capacity while the actual constraints remain.

In the earliest stage of one to five data professionals, the universal bottleneck is infrastructure. Adding data scientists before the foundation is solid produces impressive-sounding work that cannot be operationalized. At five to fifteen people, the bottleneck shifts to analytical capacity and governance. At fifteen to thirty, the organizational model begins to matter as much as individual role decisions. This is where you need to be deliberate about who owns the platform, who owns business-facing delivery, and how the two functions coordinate.

Two roles deserve specific attention. The analytics engineer, who combines data engineering skills with analytical thinking and owns the transformation layer between raw data and business-ready datasets, is consistently identified as one of the highest-leverage hires at the scaling stage. The data product manager, who owns the prioritization, roadmap, and stakeholder relationships for data products, remains underrepresented in most data organizations despite being a significant operational bottleneck that data leaders identify once their teams reach 10 or more people.

Scaling With Agents

There is a new lever for scaling a data organization beyond headcount. Agentic AI systems can independently execute bounded, well-defined tasks that would otherwise consume your data team's time or require a new hire. This is an additional capacity source, not a replacement for the operational discipline the rest of this chapter describes.

The realistic use cases today are narrow and specific. First-pass triage on incoming analytics requests, routine data quality checks that would otherwise require a person to run and interpret, a first draft of a routine report before an analyst reviews and finalizes it, answering well-scoped questions against a governed semantic layer rather than open-ended ones. What makes a task a good candidate is the same thing that makes any process a good candidate for automation. The steps are well-defined, the output is verifiable, and the cost of an occasional wrong answer is low and recoverable. Ambiguous judgment calls, anything touching a decision a business leader will act on directly, and anything where a confidently wrong answer would be expensive are not there yet, and the hallucination limitations covered in the Data Science and AI chapter do not go away just because the task is framed as agentic instead of conversational.

Do not use agents as a substitute for a hire you are avoiding making, and do not use them as a substitute for the operational discipline, monitoring, and human review any production system needs. Use them for what they are right now, a way to reclaim analyst time from routine, bounded work, so that time can go toward the judgment-heavy work only a person can do.

When to Add Your First People Leader

For a while, you manage everyone yourself, and you should. Adding a manager over a team of three or four only puts distance between you and the work for no gain. Do not create the layer before you need it.

Knowing when you need it is harder, and there is no magic number to reach for. Gallup studied more than 92,000 teams and found that the right span varies by industry, not on a fixed ratio.[70] I've found that it also varies by work complexity and quality of employees. What does hold steady is the mechanism, and that

---

[70] Gallup, "Span of Control: What's the Optimal Team Size for Managers?" gallup.com/workplace, based on a study of 92,252 teams across 104 organizations and 26 industries.

comes down to links. A link is any pairwise relationship on the team that has to stay coordinated. Two people who might disagree, duplicate work, or need to stay in sync, whether or not you are part of that conversation. A new hire adds one relationship with you, and a new potential relationship with every person already on the team. Richard Hackman showed that coordination grows far faster than headcount, following the formula n times n minus one over two, so a team of five has ten links to manage, a team of eight has 28, and a team of 12 has 66.[71] Hackman's rule was to keep headcount out of the double digits to limit links, with a preferred size of about six.

For a data leader, the binding constraint is narrower than raw span. It is coaching. You can supervise a large group; you cannot develop one. Wide spans break the individual coaching and development, because those are what a stretched manager defers. So the real signal is not headcount. It is the moment you are managing people adequately and coaching none of them, when your one-on-ones have become status updates. For complex, coaching-intensive work, that line tends to be in the mid-single digits to eight, earlier with a junior team and later with a senior one. Watch the coaching, not the org chart.

Two other signs confirm the timing. The first is that managing people starts crowding out the work only you can do, when the hours you need for strategy and stakeholders keep getting eaten

---

[71] J. Richard Hackman, Leading Teams: Setting the Stage for Great Performances (Boston: Harvard Business School Press, 2002).

by day-to-day supervision. The second is that the team splits into two clear areas of work, like engineering and analytics, and each area already has a person the others turn to for answers. When that happens, you usually already know who your first leader should be, because the best candidate is often a promotion rather than an outside hire. Promote carefully, though. Your strongest individual contributor will not automatically be your strongest leader. Managing people is a different job, and it's not a reward for being good at the old one. If the person wants it, you owe them real support through the transition.

CDO Reporting Structure

The Wavestone benchmark found that 36% of CDOs and CDAOs report to business leaders and 25% to the CIO or Chief Technology Officer (CTO),[72] with a clear trend away from CIO reporting. Data leaders who report to the CIO tend to focus on platform, infrastructure, and governance. Data leaders who report to the CEO or COO tend to focus on analytics, AI, and generating business value. The question is whether the reporting structure supports the mandate the organization needs at a given stage. Clarity of mandate matters more than the specific reporting line.

---

[72] Wavestone, 2024 Data and AI Leadership Executive Survey (Wavestone, 2024).

The rise of the Chief AI Officer adds complexity. 39% of organizations now have a CAIO,[73] and the relationship between the CDO and CAIO is unresolved in most. Organizations are solving it in different ways. If yours is navigating this question, you are in the majority.

Building an Organization That Lasts

The median CDO tenure is roughly two to three years. The most common failure modes are not technical. If your success depends entirely on one executive sponsor, you will not survive that sponsor's departure, and if you have not documented how the function operates, every personnel change will destabilize the function. The practices that extend tenure include a written mandate negotiated before you start building, measurable business outcomes documented in terms the CFO can verify, distributed executive relationships that do not collapse when any one sponsor changes roles, and a documented operating model that allows the function to continue running clearly even when the people running it change.

The goal is not to make yourself indispensable. It is to make the function indispensable.

[73] Wavestone, 2026 AI & Data Leadership Executive Benchmark Survey (Wavestone, 2026).

Leading Yourself

Everything up to this point in the chapter has been about the organization: how it scales, how it lasts, how it survives the departure of any one person, including you. But there is a person inside the role, and the number that opens the section above is telling you something uncomfortable about that person. Organizations do not churn through their data heads quickly because the work is straightforward and completed in that time. They do it because the role is hard on the people who hold it, and the expectations placed on the role are often detached from reality. Most books on data leadership will not say so.

I will. If you are going to lead a data function, you need to lead yourself first and understand what this job does to the person doing it.

Start with the isolation, because it is the part nobody warns you about. You spend your days as a translator between two worlds, and you belong fully to neither. To the engineers and scientists on your team, you have drifted away from the technical work and become one of "them," the people in meetings. To the business leaders across the table, you are still the data person, too close to the technology to be one of them. You are the one who sees both the executive hype and the operational reality, and holding both at once, alone, is wearing. Naming it helps. Finding a peer outside your organization who holds the same kind of role helps more. What does not help is pretending the weight is not there.

Then there is the pressure, which flows toward you from both directions and never stops. From above come expectations that outrun what is possible, sharpened lately by every executive who read one article about agents. From below comes the frustration of a team that is stretched and wants you to fix the conditions they are working in. Your job, much of the time, is to absorb pressure from one side, convert it into something workable, and pass a calmer version to the other. That conversion is real labor, and it draws down a reserve most leaders never think to refill.

The hardest part of protecting your capacity is that you might be capable of almost everything that lands on your desk, and that capability is the trap. You get pulled in an absurd number of directions in a single day. A strategy discussion, a vendor demo, an upset stakeholder, a candidate to interview, a board slide to write, a team conflict to mediate, and a broken dashboard that you, specifically, know how to fix because you built things like it for years. You can do all of it individually, and in many cases faster and better than anyone else on the team. But that is exactly why you have to stop yourself. The fact that you can do something is not a reason to be the one who does it.

> *A simple question does most of the work here: does this have to get done, or do you specifically have to do it?*

Watch, in particular, for the urge to jump in and save a capable person. It feels like help. It is usually harm. When you take the keyboard from an engineer who is working through a hard problem, you rob them of the struggle that would have made them better, you signal that you do not trust them to finish, and you train the whole team to escalate to you rather than work things out. A coach does not run onto the court to take the shot when a player is having a hard night. The development is in the struggle, not in being rescued from it. Your job is to make sure your people are capable and supported, and then to let them play. The discomfort of watching someone do a task at 70% of the speed or polish you would have brought is not a problem solved by doing it yourself. It is the price of building a team that can run without you, which is the team you need if you are going to last.

So delegate deliberately, and delegate the right things. Delegation done poorly is offloading the work you do not want. Delegation done well is handing someone the assignment that will stretch them, the one just past what they have done before, and then staying close enough to support them without taking it back. That is you developing your bench and protecting your bandwidth in the same move, not generosity with your time. And guard that bandwidth jealously, because a short list of things cannot be delegated at all: setting direction, securing and defending the mandate, managing up, making the priority calls, having the hardest conversations, and representing the function to the people who fund it. Those are yours alone. Every hour you spend on work someone else could have done is an hour stolen from the work only you can do, and no one else in the building will protect that time for you. You have to protect it yourself.

The value your function creates does not arrive on an executive's timeline; the honest payoff lands over 12 to 36 months, and the full return, as the value chapter will show, can take years to clear. You cannot deliver a multi-year payoff if you flame out in year one. The leader who treats the role as a sprint, answering every message at every hour and carrying the whole weight personally, is not being dedicated. They are risking that they might not be around when the work finally pays off. Protecting your own capacity is the same discipline you apply to protecting your team's, turned inward, and it is not indulgence. It is how you stay in the role long enough to matter.

There is one more shift the role demands, and it is easy to miss because nothing forces it on you. The higher you go, the farther out you have to look. An analyst thinks in days and weeks, the current sprint, the next deliverable. A manager thinks weeks and months, the roadmap, the hiring plan, the release. By the time you are running the function, your center of gravity should be twelve to thirty-six months out, where the strategy, the platform decisions, and the bench you are developing live. Nobody will tell you when to make this shift. The calendar will happily keep you at your old altitude forever, because the near-term work is concrete, urgent, and satisfying to complete, while the long-range work is ambiguous and can always wait a week. But if you are the most senior data person in the building and you are spending your thinking time on this sprint, then no one is looking at the horizon at all. That is one of the jobs that belongs to you alone. A useful audit is to ask, at the end of a normal week, how much of your attention went to anything more than ninety days away. If the answer is none, you were working in the function, and no one was leading it.

Part of leading yourself is knowing the difference between a hard stretch and a dead end, because sometimes the right move is to leave. The messy middle described earlier in this chapter is a hard stretch you push through. A structural dead end is different, and it has signals you should learn to read. Your executive sponsor leaves, and the replacement has a different vision that excludes you. The mandate you negotiated gets quietly renegotiated without your input. You notice you are spending all of your energy defending the function rather than building it. The organization has decided, in its actions if not its words, that data is a cost to be minimized rather than a capability to be grown. These are signs that the conditions the role requires have gone, and no amount of personal effort will restore them. Loyalty is a virtue. If you stay two years past the point where you can do good work, be honest about why.

And because tenure is short whether you like it or not, how you leave is part of how you lead. Everything in the section above about building an organization that lasts is also insurance for the day you walk out the door, on your terms or someone else's. Build so the function survives you. Document so your successor can continue rather than restart. Develop people who can run what you built. Do not torch the relationships or the roadmap on the way out, however the ending arrives. The truest measure of your leadership is not what the function produces while you are there. It is what it keeps producing after you are gone.

A leader who built something that collapses the moment they leave did not build as well as they thought.

There is a through-line to all of this. This book asks you to lead your people by developing them, protecting them, and getting the best from them without grinding them down. Extend the same care to the one person you are most likely to neglect, which is you. The data leaders who last are not the ones who cared least about themselves. They are the ones who understood that a depleted leader cannot lead, and who protected the one asset the entire function quietly runs on.

Further Reading

Foundational works for going deeper on this topic:

Leading Teams, by J. Richard Hackman, referenced earlier in this chapter; the research behind why team size and structure matter more than most leaders assume.

Multipliers: How the Best Leaders Make Everyone Smarter, by Liz Wiseman, a useful lens for scaling leadership itself, not just headcount, as the organization grows.

High Output Management by Andy Grove, one of the foundational texts in management generally, and specifically relevant to the leverage and coordination problems this chapter addresses.

Legacy Paper and Supply: Scaling Your Organization

You're 12 months into the role. The team has grown to eight. The branch dashboard is live across four of five branches. The demand forecasting model has completed its first full quarter in production and reduced emergency procurement orders by 34%. The customer intelligence application is in active development. The COO who arrived skeptical is now attending the monthly data review.

On the maturity curve, Legacy sits at roughly level two to three on Gartner's model, moving from Opportunistic to Systematic. On the analytics maturity curve, Legacy has moved from descriptive into predictive, with prescriptive analytics a future-state aspiration. That placement matters for the scaling decisions ahead.

By any reasonable measure, things are going well. And yet you can feel something starting to strain.

The analytics engineer is carrying three active projects simultaneously and has told you privately that she is not doing any of them as well as she would like. The data engineer is maintaining eight production pipelines while also building the new infrastructure for the customer intelligence application. The data architect has flagged two decisions made during the IDS phase for speed that are now constraints. A dimensional model design that does not scale cleanly to the 12 tables the TDS requires, and the absence of a formal data lineage process means the team cannot quickly answer where specific metrics come from. The intake queue has seventeen items. You have had to tell the COO twice in the past month that a requested analysis will take longer than expected.

The team is in the messy middle.

The instinct is to conclude that the team is understaffed and the solution is more hiring. That conclusion is often premature. Legacy's team is not understaffed relative to its current projects. It is understaffed relative to its current maintenance burden, which has been quietly accumulating for 12 months while the team focused on building new capabilities.

You do three things in response:

- **A capacity assessment**: The analytics engineer spends roughly 40% of her time on maintenance and coordination. The data engineer is spending nearly half his time on pipeline support. The data architect is spending one day a week answering lineage questions that a properly implemented data catalog would answer automatically. The team is generating new work faster than it is automating and documenting the work it has already done.

- **A technical debt remediation sprint**: You bring the proposal to the COO, a one-month period where the engineering team focuses primarily on improving the reliability of existing pipelines, implementing automated monitoring across all production tables, and beginning the data catalog work to reduce the burden of lineage questions. The projected return is a 30% reduction in maintenance time within six months. The COO approves it after some convincing. The conversation is straightforward because you have been consistently tracking and communicating operational metrics, so the maintenance burden is visible in numbers rather than anecdotes.
- **Formal documentation of the operating model is done for the first time**: The informal processes that have kept the team running for 12 months are written down. It takes two weeks and feels bureaucratic. Three months later, when contractor data engineers join to support the TDS surge work, they are fully productive within six weeks. Documentation that sits in a folder and never gets updated is not documentation. It is archaeology. You establish a simple maintenance process. Any time a process changes, the person who changed it owns the update before the sprint closes. The data architect adds a

> monthly 15-minute documentation review to the team's operating cadence, a standing agenda item in which anyone who has changed how something works confirms that it is reflected in writing. It is not glamorous. Neither is onboarding a new team member who spends their first three weeks learning that half of what is written down no longer applies.

The FinOps conversation surfaces during this period. Cloud spend has been growing at roughly 20% per quarter. Nobody has been actively managing it because the absolute numbers were small when the platform was new. They are no longer small. The data architect runs a query-optimization exercise on the ten most expensive recurring queries and reduces their compute cost by 38% without changing a single output. That finding prompts a broader cloud cost review and the establishment of a monthly FinOps practice.

The MLOps conversation surfaces at the same time. The demand forecasting model has been in production for six months and its accuracy has been drifting gradually downward as the product catalog evolved and several large customers changed their ordering patterns. Nobody set up automated accuracy monitoring when the model was deployed. The data scientist catches the drift during a routine check and retrains the model, but the incident prompts the question about what the process should be for every model going forward. Automated accuracy monitoring for every production model, a defined retraining trigger, and a named model owner responsible for responding when the trigger fires.

Three months after the remediation sprint, the team is delivering faster than before. The maintenance burden has dropped. The two contractor data engineers have joined and are productive. The data architect's lineage work has reduced the volume of weekly questions from business partners by half.

That is what scaling well looks like at Legacy. Not the ability to grow without limits, but the discipline to build something that gets more reliable as it grows, that documents itself, that manages its costs, and that is being deliberately prepared for the next phase before the next phase arrives.

The next chapter covers the value of data and insights. How to measure what the data organization produces, communicate that value in terms the business understands, and build the financial case that sustains the function through leadership changes and budget cycles.

FIFTEEN

The Value of Data and Insights

There is a scenario that plays out in organizations constantly, and it keeps playing out because nothing in the structure of most businesses prevents it.

I mentioned a version of this story briefly in the opening chapter, in the discussion of why so much data work stays invisible. It is worth telling in full here.

It goes something like this. A marketing team approaches the data organization with a request. They want a segmentation model and a propensity model to help them target customers with a campaign more precisely. The data architects make sure the infrastructure can support the volume. The data engineers source and prepare the data. The data analysts design the attribution approach and track the campaign performance. The governance team makes sure none of it runs afoul of privacy regulations. The data science team builds the models.

The campaign launches. Purchases increase by 12%. The total revenue impact is attributed at $4.2 million.

The marketing leader goes to the CEO to share the news. She presents the campaign strategy, the creative execution, and the results. The data organization is mentioned briefly, if at all. The $4.2 million gets credited to marketing. The data organization goes back to its queue.

What is wrong with this picture? Nothing, structurally. The marketing leader is doing exactly what leaders are supposed to do. She's advocating for her team and communicating the results they drove. The problem is that the data organization did not advocate for itself. It delivered the work and assumed the value would be visible. It was not. This is one of the defining challenges of data leadership. The work is real. The impact is real. But the value is structurally hidden from the people who control resources, approve budgets, and decide which functions get to grow. In most organizations, sales and marketing are viewed as value generators. Data and IT are viewed as cost centers. That perception will not change on its own. Changing it is not a nice-to-have skill for data leaders. It is a survival skill for you and your organization.

What Value Is

At its most fundamental level, value is the difference between the benefit derived from something and the cost of obtaining it. For data and analytics, neither side of that equation is standardized or easy to calculate. The accounting world recognizes three formal approaches to asset valuation: the cost approach (what it would cost to replace the asset), the market approach (what comparable assets have sold for), and the income approach (the present value of future cash flows the asset will generate). All three appear, in some form, in how data assets are valued in practice.

Several frameworks from the field are useful scaffolding. Doug Laney's *Infonomics* framework offers six models for valuing data, running from qualitative assessments of intrinsic and business value to financial calculations of cost value, market value, and economic value. MIT CISR's research identifies three modes of data monetization: Improve (using data to improve internal operations), Wrap (embedding analytics into existing products), and Sell (packaging data as an external offering). Most data organizations in their early years operate in Improve mode; understanding that Wrap and Sell represent higher rungs is useful context for a multi-year strategy.[74]

None of these frameworks needs to be introduced to your executive team by name. But understanding them shapes how you structure the value story, choose your metrics, and defend your numbers when the CFO pushes back.

---

74 **The Value of Data and Insights:** Douglas B. Laney, Infonomics: How to Monetize, Manage, and Measure Information as an Asset for Competitive Advantage (New York: Routledge, 2017); MIT Center for Information Systems Research, "Monetizing Your Data," MIT CISR Research Briefing.

The Outputs-Outcomes-Impact Distinction

Before reaching for a calculator, we need to get one conceptual distinction right, because confusing these three things is the most common reason value stories fall flat.

An **output** is what the data team produces: a trained model, a dashboard, a cleaned dataset, a governance policy. Outputs are real, deliverable, and essentially meaningless to anyone who does not work in the data organization. "We created fifteen data products, thirty-five dashboards, and eight models this year" produces a resounding shrug from leadership, with an implied or stated, "so what?"

An **outcome** is what changes for the people who use the output: decisions are made faster, fraud rates drop, the sales team spends two fewer hours per week pulling manual reports, and customer churn is identified three months earlier than before.

An **impact** is the business-level result: revenue increased, costs dropped, a regulatory penalty was avoided, a customer relationship was saved. Impacts are what executives budget around.

The logic model connects these levels: inputs (people, time, technology) drive activities (the work the data team does), which produce outputs that enable outcomes, which generate impacts. The value story lives at the impact level but must be traceable all the way back to the inputs. A data leader who says, "Our demand forecasting model reduced inventory carrying costs by $1.2 million last quarter, which more than covered the entire cost of the data engineering team," is speaking in impact terms. A data leader who says "we completed the feature engineering phase and the model is in staging" is speaking in outputs. The difference is whether the audience leaves the conversation understanding why the work matters.

Measuring Financial Value

Return on Investment is the most universally understood financial metric and the right starting point for most data initiative business cases.

$$ROI = (Benefit - Cost) / Cost \times 100$$

Cost savings and efficiency gains are often easier to calculate than revenue impact because they do not require attribution across teams. If the data organization automates a process that previously required 40 hours per week of analyst time at $75 per hour, the annual value is approximately $156,000. There's an important distinction, though. Unless the automation results in an actual reduction in headcount or budget, you have not saved $156,000. You have freed 40 hours of capacity. The more honest and more compelling version of the story is not "we saved $156,000" but "we freed the analyst team from 40 hours of manual work per week, and that capacity is now being used to complete the customer segmentation project that sales has been waiting six months for." That story is specific, visible, and connected to something the business cares about.

Risk mitigation has a probabilistic value that is frequently overlooked. If a data governance initiative reduces the likelihood of a GDPR-scale penalty from 10% to 2%, and a regulatory fine would cost the organization $5 million, the expected annual value of that risk reduction is $400,000. Most organizations undercount this category because risk-avoided costs do not appear on a P&L.

A warning on over-claiming. Measuring value primarily through dollar figures claimed is itself a Goodhart's Law trap. When data teams are evaluated on the financial value they demonstrate, accounting tends to expand. The demand forecasting model saved procurement $84,000, but it is credited in the analytics team's value report, the data engineering team's pipeline report, and the data governance team's data quality report. The numbers balloon, and the organization ends up with a data team claiming it generated $47 million in value on a $2 million budget, which strains credulity with the CFO. Measure honestly, conservatively, and with explicit assumptions a skeptical CFO could audit. Co-sign numbers with the business leaders who experienced the outcomes. A smaller, defensible number will always serve you better than a large number that falls apart under scrutiny.

Multi-Year Investments and the NPV Framework

Infrastructure investments, platform builds, and governance programs require upfront spending that generates returns over time. A simple ROI calculation is incomplete for these investments.

Net Present Value accounts for the time value of money by discounting future cash flows back to their present value. The discount rate should be the organization's weighted average cost of capital, typically between 8% and 12% for stable companies in current conditions. A data platform investment might show a negative cash flow in year one but a strongly positive NPV over five years. Walking into a CFO conversation with a five-year NPV model signals that you speak the language of investment rather than the language of spending.

The Attribution Problem

The marketing scenario at the opening of this chapter is the attribution problem in its most visible form. How should a $4.2 million outcome be allocated when two teams each contributed?

Equal credit is the simplest approach: both teams contributed, both teams share the outcome equally. Simple, but ignores the reality that contributions are rarely equal.

Weighted contribution is more defensible. Each team's contribution is assessed based on the specific work it performed and the total value allocated proportionally. It requires judgment and negotiation but produces a more honest accounting.

Incremental value is the most rigorous. The question it asks: How much additional revenue did each team generate beyond what would have happened without them? If a generic campaign had generated $2 million, the incremental lift of $2.2 million is being allocated, and each team's share is the portion attributable to its specific contribution.

The most important rule is to negotiate the attribution framework before the project starts, not after. The worst time to discuss how credit will be split is when a campaign has just succeeded and both teams are in the room with the CEO. At that point, every attribution conversation feels like a turf war. The right time is project kickoff, when the data organization and the business team are aligning on scope and success criteria. Document the agreement. Involve Finance as the neutral arbiter. Data leaders who build this practice into their operating model systematically avoid the invisible-work problem, because credit is no longer an afterthought. It is a project deliverable.

None of this is easy, and if you have never seen a formal attribution negotiation happen at project kickoff, you are not alone. Most organizations never have this conversation explicitly. The organizations that manage this well are the exception, and if you are the first person to propose it at yours, expect some resistance framed as "Why are we talking about credit before we've even built anything?" This process will never happen on its own. Someone must build it into how projects start.

Communicating Value to Non-Technical Audiences

The CFO needs ROI, NPV, and payback period. The VP of Sales needs to understand how the model affected their pipeline and win rate. The COO needs operational efficiency gains in terms of cycle time and error rates. The CEO needs the headline and the strategic implication. One value story presented identically to all four will land with none of them.

This is not a skill you can keep to yourself. I once asked an analyst to write a short email to a business partner summarizing the impact of an analysis he had just finished. He pushed back, with a laugh, "I'm not a salesman." I told him, half-joking myself, "Yes you are. We all are." Every person on a data team is doing work that will stay invisible unless someone describes what it accomplished, and waiting for that description to come from you alone does not scale past a team of one. Teaching your analysts to write two honest sentences about the impact of their own work, not a sales pitch, just a clear statement of what changed and why it mattered, is one of the highest-leverage things you can build into how the team operates.

Maintain an internal master value-tracking document and develop audience-specific summaries from it. The underlying numbers are the same. The emphasis, the format, and the level of technical detail change.

Lead with the business result, not the technical approach. Use one or two clear visualizations rather than 12 slides of charts. State recommendations or requests explicitly rather than leaving the audience to draw their own conclusions. And be short enough to fit into the first ten minutes of a thirty-minute meeting.

Treat value communication as a practice, not an event. Quarterly updates, a running scorecard of data initiative outcomes that business leaders can see on demand, and proactively sharing relevant results with the specific leaders who care about them. These practices, maintained consistently, are what shift the perception from cost center to value creator.

Turning Value Into Budget

Proving value and communicating it are necessary, but they are not the finish line. The place where all that work either pays off or evaporates is the annual budget cycle. This is the arena. A leader who can build an elegant NPV case but still cannot navigate budget season will see the function cut anyway.

The value story is the ammunition and the budget cycle is the fight.

The first thing to understand is that budgeting is a cycle, not an event, and it runs on a calendar you need to learn and get ahead of. By the time the official request is due, the real decisions have usually been shaped already, in informal conversations weeks earlier. The leaders who win budget do the work before the deadline. They seed the value story with stakeholders through the year, align with their sponsor before the numbers are locked, and make sure the CFO has heard about the wins long before they see the ask. Showing up cold to budget season with a strong case and no groundwork is how good functions lose to weaker ones that managed their relationships better. This is the managing-up discipline applied to money.

When you do make the ask, frame it in the language of outcomes, not costs. "I need two more engineers" is a cost, and costs get cut. "For $300,000 I can extend the forecasting capability to two more business units, which operations values at roughly $200,000 a year in reduced emergency orders and stockouts" is an investment, and investments get funded. This is the outputs-outcomes-impact distinction and the translation discipline applied to your own budget. Tie every dollar you request to a use case and, wherever you can, to a business owner who will co-sign the number. A budget line the business co-owns is far harder to cut than one the data team defends alone.

Headcount is the largest and least reversible part of that ask, so plan it against the roadmap rather than against ambition. Sequence hires to your actual bottlenecks, the same discipline covered in the scaling chapter, and be honest with yourself about what each one commits you to.

Every permanent hire is a standing liability, not a one-time purchase.

A leader who staffs up aggressively in a strong year with no plan for a lean one is building a trap they will step into later. Use contractors for true surges and reserve permanent hires for durable needs. Keep protecting the operational capacity discussed earlier, because a team budgeted to the last hour has no room to absorb the work that does not fit a plan.

At some point, often when you least expect it, you will be told to cut, or to do more with less. How you handle that moment defines you more than any growth year. There are two easy failures. The first is cutting the invisible defensive work first, because it is the easiest to cut and nobody screams when it goes. That is exactly the trap the data management chapter warned about. Defensive work is invisible when it is working, so it looks painless to cut, and the damage shows up months later as the incidents and errors it was quietly preventing. The second failure is slicing everything equally, which leaves every capability a little broken and none of them working. The better path is to protect the core capabilities on which everything else depends, cut the low-value work you have been meaning to kill anyway, and be transparent with your stakeholders about what the cut removes. Make the trade visible, the same way you do when you say no to a request: name what the organization is giving up, so the consequence is owned by the business rather than absorbed silently by your team. Never mortgage the future to survive the quarter without saying out loud that this is what you are doing.

Every leader in this position eventually wants to grow the function, and the incentives pointing that direction are real, not vanity. It is good for you; more scope and responsibility is how careers advance. It is good for your people; a growing function has more room for promotion and more interesting problems to work on. And if you genuinely believe the function creates outsized value, growing it is the right call for the business too.

But growth is not free, and it creates risks a smaller function never has to think about. The most obvious one: growth makes you visible in a way that invites scrutiny you did not have before. A team of six rarely gets a hard look from the board. A team of thirty, with a budget line an executive dashboard tracks by name, becomes an obvious target the next time the company is looking for something to cut, and the same visibility that got you the resources is what puts you in that conversation. There is also a coordination cost most leaders underestimate. The same math from the scaling chapter (a team of twelve carrying 66 coordination links instead of a team of six carrying 15) can affect culture and quality. A bigger team is a fundamentally different, harder job to lead, not just a larger version of the same one.

Growth can also become the goal itself rather than a means to one; a leader praised for the size of the team they built starts optimizing for headcount instead of the value that headcount was supposed to produce. And growing is asymmetric with shrinking. Adding eight people over two good years feels like momentum. Losing three of them in one bad year, for reasons that may have nothing to do with performance, reads as failure regardless of how sound the underlying decision was. Grow deliberately, not reflexively, and know before you ask for the next hire whether you could defend having them if the year ahead turns out to be a hard one.

Budget season is where the distinction that opened this chapter, cost center versus value center, stops being a talking point and becomes real money. Treat it as a chore you endure once a year and you will re-fight for the function's survival every year, no matter how good the work is. Treat it as the recurring moment when the value you created converts into the resources to create more, and the function compounds; each year's delivered value funds a larger ask, which in turn funds more value. That compounding, not any single ROI number, is what a well-run data organization looks like from the finance side of the table.

Further Reading

Foundational works for going deeper on this topic:

Infonomics, by Douglas B. Laney, referenced earlier in this chapter; the fuller case for treating information itself as a measurable, monetizable asset.

How to Measure Anything: Finding the Value of Intangibles in Business, by Douglas W. Hubbard, a rigorous, practical answer to the objection that some kinds of value simply can't be quantified.

Legacy Paper and Supply: Measuring Value

18 months into building the data organization at Legacy, the value question surfaces in a way that makes its urgency impossible to ignore. The CFO requests a meeting. She has been reviewing departmental budgets and wants to understand what the data organization has produced relative to the cost. The question is not hostile. It is the question every data function eventually faces, and if you cannot answer it specifically, you will not have the function for long.

The preparation for that meeting reveals a gap that should have been closed much earlier. Projects have been delivered, results have flowed to the business teams that requested them, and nobody has been systematically tracking what any of it was worth. The data organization has been operating in outputs, delivering models, dashboards, pipelines, and governance policies without connecting those outputs to outcomes and impacts in a documented, communicable form. That changes today.

The Retrospective Value Inventory

The first task is to go back over the last 12 months and document three things for each significant initiative. What the data organization delivered, what changed for the business as a result, and the dollar impact. Output, outcome, impact.

The branch dashboard produces two value streams:

- **Efficiency**: 15 sales representatives saving two hours per week at a fully loaded cost of $60 per hour produce approximately $93,600 in annual time savings.
- **Account retention**: The dashboard's activity alerts prompted proactive retention conversations, protecting accounts worth approximately $156,000 in annual revenue in its first year.

Total year one value is approximately $250,000. That number is built with the VP of Sales in the room, using his estimates of account values and his team's assessment of which retention conversations the dashboard enabled. The value story is more credible when the business partner co-signs the numbers.

The demand forecasting model is the strongest value story in the inventory. Legacy's procurement spend runs approximately $28 million annually. Emergency orders accounted for roughly 4% of procurement spend, each carrying an average premium of 22% above standard cost, resulting in a baseline emergency premium cost of approximately $246,000 annually. The model reduced emergency orders by 34% in its first quarter, generating approximately $84,000 in first-year savings. The COO and head of procurement verify the assumptions and co-sign the estimate.

The customer intelligence application is still in pilot with no realized dollar value yet. Rather than leaving it out, you build a prospective estimate: 40 sales representatives saving one hour per week at 65 dollars per hour produces approximately $135,000 in annual value in its first full year. Presented as a projection with assumptions clearly stated, not as a realized figure.

What the Numbers Cannot Capture

Before presenting the financial story, you add something the CFO did not ask for but needs to hear.

The governance program has established, for the first time in Legacy's history, a single, agreed-upon definition of an active customer. Sales, finance, and the CRM now produce the same number. That sounds small. It is not. Every significant commercial decision Legacy's leadership makes from this point forward is based on a shared understanding of who the customer is. The value of that consistency compounds over time in ways that cannot be attributed to any single initiative.

The data platform itself is an asset that did not exist 18 months ago. Its value is not the work it has already done. It is the work it makes possible.

The Five-Year NPV Case

You bring something else to the meeting: a five-year NPV model that shows what the investment is expected to produce over the full useful life of the capabilities being built.

The model uses a 10% discount rate, consistent with Legacy's weighted average cost of capital. Costs are $1.5 million in year one and $1.1 million annually in years two through five. Benefits are built use case by use case, with assumptions documented and co-signed by the relevant business leaders.

Year one total benefits: $370,000. Net cash flow: negative $1,130,000. Expected and planned.

Year two total benefits: $735,000, with the customer intelligence application contributing $175,000 in its first full year of production. Net cash flow: negative $365,000. The loss is narrowing.

Year three is the inflection point. Total benefits reach $1,725,000, including $750,000 from additional TDS use cases now delivering value across sales, operations, and finance. Net cash flow turns positive at $625,000.

Year four total benefits: $2,175,000. Year five: $2,675,000. The growth reflects the compounding nature of a maturing data organization. As more use cases come online, as AI capabilities reach full production, and as data literacy improves, the value generated per dollar of investment increases.

Applying the 10% discount rate, the five-year NPV is positive $853,000. The initial investment is recovered within approximately 46 months of the TDS approval.

The CFO's first question is about the additional TDS use cases in year three. What specifically is included, and how were the estimates derived? You open the appendix, which contains a one-page summary of each use case, the business leader who sponsored it, the estimated value, and the assumptions behind the estimate. Every number has a name attached to it. That level of specificity is what makes a financial model credible rather than aspirational.

The Attribution Conversation

The retrospective inventory reveals another uncomfortable finding. The operations manager who used the data organization's inventory analysis to inform a supplier renegotiation that saved $400,000 credits his own judgment for the outcome. He is not wrong. His judgment was what turned the analysis into action. But the data organization's contribution is invisible in any record that matters.

You commit to a practice going forward, begin the attribution conversation before the project starts rather than after it delivers results. Align with the relevant business leader on how success will be measured, the data organization's contribution, and how credit will be allocated. Involve Finance as the neutral arbiter where possible.

In practice, this will not always work. Some business leaders will not want to share credit before they know whether there is credit to share. You cannot force the conversation. But you can make it a standard part of how every project kicks off, ask the question, document what is agreed, and build a track record of delivering outcomes that make the attribution argument harder to dismiss over time.

The CFO closes the meeting the way she closes most meetings: efficiently. The numbers are stronger than she expected. She wants this methodology carried forward and an updated model at the six-month mark.

It is a quiet ending to a meeting that required months of preparation. But something has changed. The data organization walked into this room as a cost center defending its budget. It is leaving as a function with a documented track record, a credible financial model, and a CFO who now has a basis for advocating for it in conversations you will never be in. That shift will show up every time someone at the leadership table asks whether the data investment is worth it, and the CFO already knows the answer.

The next chapter covers the future of data organizations. Where the field is heading, which capabilities will define competitive advantage over the next decade, and what it means to lead effectively in a world where tools, talent, and business expectations are all changing simultaneously.

SIXTEEN

The Future of Data Organizations

The data landscape has always been complex and always been changing. The tools that defined best practice five years ago are being replaced. The roles that did not exist a decade ago are now foundational. What is new is the pace of change and the magnitude.

AI has dialed everything up. Nobody knows with confidence what the data professional's toolkit will look like in five years. Anyone who claims that kind of precision is either more confident than the evidence warrants or selling something. What has not changed, and will not change, is the importance of the fundamentals. The organizations that navigate this period well will be those that have kept their governance programs current, their data quality high, their engineering foundations sound, and their teams developing.

The Adoption Surge and the Value Gap

McKinsey's State of AI research found that the share of organizations using AI in at least one business function has climbed to roughly 78%, up from 55% two years earlier.[75] And yet, only roughly 6% qualify as AI high performers, capturing meaningful, measurable EBIT impact. The Wavestone and DataIQ 2025 survey found that only 46% of organizations report high or significant business value from their data and AI investments, despite 98% increasing investment.[76]

Nearly everyone has adopted AI. Almost no one has captured durable value from it.

This is not a technology problem. The models are good enough. The infrastructure is accessible enough. The problem is organizational. Organizations that have not built the foundational data capabilities, governance structures, talent, culture, and leadership alignment needed to translate technology into business outcomes. The gap between adoption and value capture is, at its core, a leadership and organizational problem. Which means it is exactly the kind of problem that the readers of this book are positioned to solve.

[75] **The Future of Data Organizations:** McKinsey & Company, "The State of AI in 2025," McKinsey Global Survey.

[76] Wavestone and DataIQ, 2025 AI & Data Leadership Executive Benchmark Survey.

Agentic AI: The Most Important Shift Happening Right Now

Generative AI was the beginning of a story, not the whole story. The more consequential development for data organizations is agentic AI.

An AI agent does not wait for a prompt. It plans and executes multi-step workflows autonomously, using tools, APIs, and data to take actions on behalf of a user or a business process. Instead of generating a summary when asked, an agent monitors a data pipeline, identifies an anomaly, cross-references it against historical patterns, drafts an incident report, and routes it to the right person without being asked.

Enterprise adoption of task-specific AI agents is accelerating rapidly, with industry forecasts projecting a rise from under 5% of applications in 2025 toward roughly 40% within a few years. Gartner has also issued an important caution: over 40% of agentic AI projects are expected to be canceled due to escalating costs, unclear business value, and inadequate risk controls.[77] The hype is real, and it will lead to real failures. That does not change the underlying trajectory.

[77] Gartner, "Gartner Predicts Over 40% of Agentic AI Projects Will Be Canceled by End of 2027," press release, 2025.

For data organizations specifically, agentic AI creates three immediate implications:

- **Infrastructure:** Agents are not consumers of dashboards. They are consumers of real-time, reliable, well-documented data products with stable APIs and clear contracts. An agent cannot navigate a poorly governed data environment any better than a human analyst can; it just fails faster and at greater scale. Organizations that have invested in data quality, cataloging, and data product thinking will be positioned to unlock agentic value. Those who have not will find that agents simultaneously expose every weakness in their data foundation.
- **Governance:** When data users were humans reading dashboards, governance meant access control and data quality standards. When agents are autonomous actors taking actions on behalf of the business, governance means something broader: what an agent is permitted to do, how its actions are audited, and who is accountable when an agent makes a consequential error. These questions do not yet have established answers, and the organizations building those answers now are developing a capability that will matter enormously within the next few years.
- **Organizational design:** If agents handle an increasing share of routine analytical work, the composition of what a data organization does shifts. Fewer people

writing routine SQL. More people designing the systems agents operate within, evaluating agent outputs, maintaining the data products agents consume, and governing the processes agents execute.

The work changes before the headcount does.

The Modern Data Stack Is Consolidating

The dominant approach to building a data platform was to assemble best-of-breed tools. One vendor for ingestion, another for transformation, another for orchestration, another for warehousing, another for governance. This gave organizations flexibility and access to best-in-class capabilities at each layer. It also gave them complexity, integration debt, and a growing list of vendor relationships to manage.

That era is ending. The three major cloud providers, AWS, Microsoft Azure, and Google Cloud, are each building or acquiring the capabilities to offer a comprehensive, integrated data platform. Microsoft Fabric brings together data engineering, data warehousing, data science, real-time analytics, and business intelligence under a single product with unified governance. Google Cloud offers BigQuery, Vertex AI, Looker, and Dataplex. AWS offers the deepest portfolio of individual services, moving toward tighter integration through AWS Data Zone and related governance offerings.

The choice of cloud provider is increasingly a strategic decision. An organization already running on Microsoft 365 and Azure has a natural path to Microsoft Fabric. A Google-native organization has a natural path to BigQuery and Vertex AI. Switching costs between them are high enough that the decision made today will shape the data platform for years to come.

The Regulatory Environment Is Becoming Binding

For most of the history of data organizations, regulation was managed primarily by legal and compliance teams. That is changing, and the change is now operational rather than theoretical.

The EU AI Act is the world's most comprehensive AI governance framework. Data leaders need to know the timeline. Prohibited practices, including certain biometric surveillance and social scoring systems, were banned as of February 2025. General-purpose AI model obligations took effect in August 2025. High-risk AI systems, including AI used in employment, credit scoring, educational admissions, critical infrastructure, law enforcement, and healthcare, came fully into scope in August 2026. Penalties can reach up to 35 million euros or 7% of global annual turnover, whichever is higher. For organizations doing business with or in

Europe, that deadline has already reshaped what an AI governance program needs to cover.[78]

Two frameworks should be on every data leader's mind. The NIST AI Risk Management Framework, published in January 2023, organizes AI risk management around four functions: Govern, Map, Measure, and Manage. It is increasingly being written into state laws, procurement requirements, and industry standards as the de facto baseline for responsible AI practice. NIST AI 600-1, published in July 2024, is the companion profile specifically addressing generative AI risks. It names 12 specific risk categories including hallucination and confabulation, prompt injection, data poisoning, privacy leakage, and over-reliance. For any organization deploying large language models in production, this document describes the risk landscape the governance program needs to address.[79]

Positioning your organization as the home for responsible AI deployment, bringing the same rigor to AI governance that the function brings to data quality and lineage, makes the function more central to how the business operates and builds influence that outlasts any single technology cycle.

---

[78] European Union, Regulation (EU) 2024/1689 (Artificial Intelligence Act), Official Journal of the European Union, July 12, 2024.

[79] National Institute of Standards and Technology, AI Risk Management Framework: Generative Artificial Intelligence Profile (NIST AI 600-1), July 2024.

Governance Is Being Rebuilt for a Different World

The governance challenges posed by generative and agentic AI go beyond what traditional data governance frameworks were designed to address.

Traditional data governance addressed structured data in defined systems. Who owns which table, what the quality standards are, who can access what, and how long it is retained. Generative AI introduces problems that lack direct analogs in that framework. Hallucination is not a data quality problem in the traditional sense. There is no pipeline to fix. Governance for hallucination means establishing evaluation frameworks, output validation processes, and human-review requirements for high-stakes outputs, rather than assuming model outputs are accurate. Prompt injection, where adversarial input causes a model to take unintended actions, is a security and governance problem that did not exist in the world of SQL queries and dashboards. Training data lineage and the copyright and consent status of data used to train models have become consequential legal questions.

McKinsey's 2025 survey found that 47% of organizations had experienced at least one negative consequence of generative AI, with inaccuracy and intellectual property leakage as the top two incidents. Shadow AI, where employees use personal AI tools for work without organizational knowledge or consent, has emerged as a governance gap reported across the large majority of organizations.

The data leader who treats these as someone else's problem is misreading their role. These governance questions require exactly the combination of technical depth, organizational authority, and business judgment that a mature data organization provides.

The Evolving Role of the Data Leader

Gartner's 2025 CDAO Agenda Survey found that 70% of CDAOs now have primary responsibility for AI strategy and operating model, a significant expansion from their traditional role. The percentage reporting directly to the CEO reached 36% in 2025, up from 21% in 2024.[80] Data leadership is being pulled toward the center of business strategy. The troubling counterpart. Gartner also predicts that 75% of CDAOs not seen as essential to their organization's AI success will eventually lose their C-level positions.[81]

Gartner identifies three archetypes diverging from the original CDO role. The Expert is the recognized enterprise authority on platforms, governance, and infrastructure, with depth in technical and operational data management. The Connector bridges C-suite and technical teams, embeds analytics into products and

[80] Gartner, "Gartner Survey Finds 70% of CDAOs Are Responsible for AI Strategy and Operating Model," press release, May 12, 2025, based on the Gartner CDAO Agenda Survey for 2025 (504 data and analytics leaders, surveyed September–November 2024).

[81] Gartner, "Gartner Survey Finds 70% of CDAOs Are Responsible for AI Strategy and Operating Model," press release, May 12, 2025.

decisions, and focuses on making the rest of the organization more capable. The Pioneer owns data, AI, and analytics as an integrated portfolio and operates as a genuine business strategy partner at the senior leadership table.

The passive, internally focused data leader who manages platforms and waits to be asked for help is not one of the three viable futures. The data leader of 2030 is externally oriented, business-fluent, and accountable for outcomes rather than outputs.

Human-AI Collaboration and What It Means for Data Careers

Some things AI is doing right now that data professionals used to do include writing routine SQL queries, building simple dashboards, generating first-draft documentation, producing standard reports, and cleaning and reformatting data. These tasks won't disappear everywhere overnight. They'll gradually become things AI assists with, rather than things humans do from scratch.

What AI cannot do reliably is connect data analysis to business strategy with judgment, navigate organizational politics to get good data work used, earn the trust of a skeptical executive, evaluate whether an AI-generated output is reasonable before it reaches a business stakeholder, or take accountability when something goes wrong. These are human capabilities that become increasingly valuable as AI handles more mechanical work.

The pattern of history with technology transitions is consistent. Automation displaces specific tasks, not entire professions, and creates demand for new capabilities. The World Economic Forum's Future of Jobs Report 2025 projects that by 2030, 170 million new jobs will be created globally while 92 million are displaced, for a net increase of 78 million.[82] Big data specialists and AI and machine learning specialists are among the three fastest-growing roles. Data entry clerks are among the fastest declining.

The practical guidance is straightforward. Use AI aggressively to do more with less, and invest deliberately in the human capabilities AI cannot replicate. Judgment in ambiguous situations, organizational understanding, the ability to earn trust from skeptical partners, and the skill of connecting technical work to business outcomes. These compound over a career in ways that no tool upgrade can match. The data professionals who combine both, who are fluent in the tools and exceptional at the human work, are the ones who will define what this field looks like a decade from now.

For those in or approaching leadership, the mandate is expanding whether you asked for it or not. Positioning your organization as the home for responsible AI deployment, bringing the same rigor

---

[82] World Economic Forum, Future of Jobs Report 2025 (Geneva: World Economic Forum, January 2025).

to AI governance that the function brings to data quality and lineage, makes the function more central to how the business operates. The one who treats AI as someone else's problem will find themselves explaining why their function matters while the AI agenda happens around them.

Further Reading

Foundational works for going deeper on this topic:

Co-Intelligence: Living and Working with AI, by Ethan Mollick, a clear-eyed, practical guide to working alongside AI rather than either dismissing it or overselling it.

The Coming Wave, by Mustafa Suleyman, a co-founder of DeepMind, on the harder question this chapter only gestures at: what happens when this technology's trajectory keeps compounding.

Legacy Paper and Supply: A Look Ahead

You have been at Legacy long enough now to have seen what the organization was and to understand what it could become.

When you arrived, Legacy had data but not a data organization. It had reports but not insights. It had talent but not a strategy. None of that is true anymore. The data organization you have built has a strategy that connects to the business, processes that make work repeatable, people who understand their roles, a value-measurement practice that makes contributions visible, and relationships with business partners who now come to the data team with problems rather than specifications.

What comes next will test all of it in ways the work so far has not.

The agentic AI conversation is already starting at Legacy. An executive attended a conference last month and came back asking whether Legacy could deploy agents to automate customer outreach. Someone in operations wants an agent that monitors inventory and automatically triggers reorders. These are not unreasonable requests. The problem is sequencing. Agents consume real-time, well-documented data products with stable APIs and clear contracts. Legacy's foundation is solid for its current use cases. It is not yet ready for agents taking autonomous actions. The governance frameworks for what agents are permitted to do, how their actions are audited, and who is accountable when an agent makes a consequential error have not been formally built. Your job in these conversations is to say not yet, but here's how we get there.

The platform consolidation happening in the market is already a Legacy decision. The tooling choices made during the IDS phase were made for speed and the team's existing skill set. The Fivetran and dbt Labs merger, Snowflake's expansion into orchestration and AI, Databricks' addition of agent infrastructure: these are not abstract market trends. They will change what the tools Legacy uses today look like in three years. The semantic layer question is particularly relevant. As the customer intelligence application approaches full production and agentic AI conversations intensify, a single governed definition of every queryable business concept becomes infrastructure rather than a nice-to-have. The data architect needs to include the platform architecture review in the next planning cycle agenda.

The regulatory environment is not a future concern for Legacy. Legacy does not currently deploy AI systems in the EU AI Act's high-risk categories. But the NIST AI Risk Management Framework currently applies to the customer intelligence application. The application gives sales representatives direct natural language access to customer data. The governance frameworks for hallucination risk, the process for validating outputs before they reach end users, and the accountability structure for when the application produces an incorrect answer have not been formally implemented. Close that gap before full production rollout, not after.

Shadow AI is already present at Legacy, whether anyone has acknowledged it or not. Several sales representatives have mentioned using public AI tools to draft customer emails and summarize account histories. Treating this as a policy violation alone will drive it underground. Treating it as information about unmet demand will find you more use cases for the TDS pipeline.

Your role at Legacy is expanding whether the title changes or not. You have been operating as a Connector since the first listening tour with business leaders. The agentic AI conversations, the regulatory questions, the platform consolidation decisions: all of these are pushing toward Pioneer territory. That is not a promotion to ask for. It is a responsibility to step into by demonstrating that the data organization is the right home for Legacy's AI strategy, not only its data infrastructure.

The team at Legacy is facing the human-AI collaboration question directly. The two data analysts are spending meaningful time on work that AI tools are already beginning to automate. You owe them an honest conversation about what their roles will look like in three years and what skills they should be building now. AI engineering, data product management, and AI governance are the growth tracks most likely to be durable. Building development paths toward those tracks for people who are currently writing SQL and building dashboards is both a retention practice and an organizational capability investment.

What comes next at Legacy is not a new chapter. It is the same chapter, with harder questions.

The data organizations that will define the next era are the ones that close the gap between AI adoption and AI value capture. Legacy has the foundation to be one of them. Whether it becomes one will depend on the same things it has always depended on. Leadership that stays connected to what the business needs, a team that keeps building the right capabilities in the right order, and a data leader who refuses to let the function's contribution remain invisible.

The foundation you have built is not the ceiling. It is the floor. What gets built on top of it, and whether it lasts, depends on your ability to focus on what drives the business forward, and your ability to embrace and champion change.

A Letter to the Reader

Thank you for reading this book.

If you have made it this far, you are serious about this work. That matters, because this work is serious. The businesses that figure out how to build and lead data organizations that deliver value will have a meaningful advantage over the ones that do not.

I hope you do not feel overwhelmed by everything this book covers. If you do, that is understandable. Data leadership is complex, and the landscape it operates in is changing faster than any single book can fully capture. There is a lot here. You will not do it all at once, and you should not try.

What you can do is show up tomorrow and make your data organization just a little bit better than it was today. Fix the governance gap that has been bothering you. Have the feedback conversation you have been putting off. Clean up the pipeline that has been running on hope and manual intervention for six months. Build the relationship with the skeptical business partner. Document the process that only you know how to run. None of those things are dramatic. All of them compound.

The leaders who build great data organizations do not do it in a single inspired sprint. They do it through thousands of small, deliberate improvements made over time, through hiring people they trust and developing them well, through earning the organization's confidence one delivered commitment at a time, and through staying curious about what is coming next without losing sight of what still needs to be done today.

That is the whole game.

The best data leaders are not always the ones with the most experience or the greatest technical skills. They are the ones who want to lead, who take the responsibility seriously enough to prepare for it, who care about the people they are building with and the organizations they are building for. The fact that you picked up this book tells me you are one of those people.

If I could sit across from you right now, I would tell you what I tell every student in my course at the end of the semester. Don't worry if you don't feel like you know everything yet. No one does. But I hope this has given you a framework to think about the work and enough knowledge to ask great questions. Keep learning.

Now go jump in. I'm rooting for you.

- Steven

About the Author

Steven Jordan is a data leader, educator, and practitioner with more than a decade of experience building and leading data organizations in some of the most demanding business environments.

He currently serves as Head of IT Data and Analytics at The Vanguard Group, one of the world's largest investment management companies, where he leads teams and capabilities that turn data into business value at enterprise scale. Before Vanguard, Steven built and led data organizations at American Airlines, Ingersoll Rand, and Driven Brands, giving him firsthand experience with the full range of challenges this book addresses: the politics of getting a data strategy funded, the difficulty of hiring in a competitive market, the frustration of delivering real value that goes unrecognized, and the specific complexity of leading a function that most of the organization does not fully understand.

Steven designed and teaches a graduate course at the University of North Carolina at Charlotte called Building and Leading Data Organizations, one of the few courses of its kind in the country. The course, and this book, grew from a conviction that data initiative failure is primarily a leadership problem, not a technical one, and that the field desperately needed a resource that addressed both the what and the how of leading in data.

He holds a master's degree in data science and business analytics from The University of North Carolina at Charlotte and is a Certified Data Management Professional through DAMA International. Before his career in data, Steven served in the United States Army as a member of the Old Guard, the Army's official ceremonial unit, where he led infantry soldiers and earned the Army Achievement Medal for leadership.

He lives in the Charlotte, North Carolina, area with his wife, Allyson, and their two children.

Index

www.ingramcontent.com/pod-product-compliance
Lightning Source LLC
LaVergne TN
LVHW010711061126
851857LV00014B/1142
* 9 7 9 8 8 9 8 1 6 1 6 5 1 *